VIEWPOINT ON
SOUTH AFRICA

VIEWPOINT ON SOUTH AFRICA

... a call for reason.

Dewar McCormack

CONTENTS

INTRODUCTION

The chapters in this book developed from a full-length autobiographical reminiscence in which I look back over my broadcasting career and recall people I have interviewed and places I have visited.

In the process of writing, I found myself taking stock of my position as a South African and particularly as an English-speaking South African. Where do we fit into the overall South African historical and contemporary picture? For the benefit of the overseas reader who does not know this country, let me explain that the term "English-speaking South African" is applied rather loosely to a White South African whose antecedents are largely Anglo-Saxon, though the English language in South Africa is shared by Afrikaners, Coloured and Black South Africans, those of Asian descent, and immigrants.

Gradually what I was writing drifted into the political sphere, though this was not the original intention. However, as hardly anything in our country escapes being dubbed "political", this is understandable! In consequence, these chapters are likely to be judged "controversial", a word I dislike for being undefinitive. At one stage of my broadcasting career, I was regarded as a "controversial personality", another term that is usually applied loosely and inaccurately. The reason for my being branded, so to speak, was that in a number of broadcasts I had tried to look at South African affairs from a standpoint other than the popular line usually touted among us English-speakers. I tended to question the stereotypes that are so easily built up, whereby one person is a "goodie" and the other a "baddie". On personal acquaintance, I have often found these stereotypes dangerously inaccurate.

I have to thank the South African Broadcasting Corporation for their agreement to my using extracts from recordings that I have made, and naturally I am grateful to interviewees both here and abroad who gave me excellent material. Inevitably I have had to select only a comparatively few, which means that I could not include others who had pertinent things to say. In making a selection, I was struck by the fact that although the recordings were taped quite a few years ago in some cases, the views expressed still have contemporary validity. A further point needs to be made that all interviewees spoke "off the cuff"; what I have included are verbatim, unedited extracts. Also, it is important to understand that I did not seek these interviews with a South African context in mind; the fact that some of the remarks have a bearing on current circumstances is purely coincidental.

My thanks also to publishers who gave me permission to quote from their published works. The titles and other details appear in the text.

It will be noted that, in referring to Black people, I have used a capital "B". I feel this is logical in recognising these groups as significant entities – and as a courtesy.

I hope that readers, particularly those abroad, may get a better idea of – and a more accurate perspective on – South Africa from these seven chapters.

Cape Town
October 1987

Dewar McCormack

BOER AND BRIT

An historical background in brief

My first sight of England could not have been more dramatic – or emotional. It was from the upper gun turret of a
four-engined R.A.F. bomber in which a party of released
prisoners-of-war were being ferried out of Europe in May
1945.

I had been in a camp in the former Sudetenland, outside
a small town named Brüx, and a Soviet flying column on its
way to capture Prague had fought one of the last engage-
ments of the war right outside our camp, and we were "out
of the bag". From there in railway trucks to Pilsen with an
overnight stop at the famous Karlsbad spa where we swam
in the river (what a delight that was) and where I and a
couple of mates cadged a bed from two old ladies living
alone in a big house who were absolutely terrified. They
provided an excellent meal despite the shortage of food, and
we slept on feather beds. The whole thing was like a picnic
– we were free and the weather was glorious and we sang as
we stood in those open trucks on the way to Pilsen.

From there the United States Air Force flew us to Rheims
and from there the R.A.F. ferried us over to an airfield near
Horsham in Sussex. We were packed like sardines into this
bomber, and I remember squatting for most of the flight
with my nose pressed up against some electronic apparatus.
The captain of the aircraft very thoughtfully arranged that
we should go up one by one into the upper gun turret to
have a look-see, and when my turn came we were over the
English Channel and I looked out and, unbelievably, there
were the white cliffs of Dover, almost the symbol of an England that I had heard about and read so much about, and
dreamed of, but had never visited. That's why I say it was an
emotional moment.

Many of us English-speaking South Africans, though we may share an inheritance from the various population strains that came to this country – Dutch, French, German, Portuguese, and Irish in my case – have been brought up in what used to be an essentially English way – or that is what we thought. I was nurtured on English history, fables, famous novels like *Vanity Fair*, popular magazines like the *Boy's Own Paper* and the *Magnet* and the *Gem*, and I knew all about Harry Wharton and Billy Bunter and the goings on at Greyfriars School. So, automatically, I absorbed a respect for English tradition, respect for the monarchy, an appreciation of a sense of fair play, and the ability (I thought) to differentiate between gentlemen and cads.

Looking back from this vantage point of experience, although it may seem rather over-exaggerated, we did pick up some values. But I do blush to think that for quite a number of years while South Africa was part of the Commonwealth and we listened to the monarch's Christmas Day broadcast, on the playing of the national anthem at the end, I used to get out of my chair and stand to attention.

I am certainly not alone in this early and sustained addiction to things British, and I have every sympathy with my Afrikaans fellow countryman for being irked for what he has taken (not always justifiably) as a lack of commitment to South Africa, our own country. But, of course, we do have a substantial proportion of British-descended people in this country, apart from the big wave of post-war immigration.

I would venture the view, curious as it might strike one, that of all the countries of the old Empire and the new Commonwealth, South Africa has perhaps a more abiding regard (and even affection) for Britain than any of the others. I would include the Afrikaner in this, broadly speaking though naturally with exceptions. When overseas, the Afrikaner will find himself at home not in Amsterdam or the Hague, nor in Paris (even if his name is du Plessis or Roux), nor in Berlin, but in London.

Rather in the way that the convert to Catholicism can be more intense about his faith than the born Roman Catholic, so it could well be argued that more than a few English-speaking South Africans are as concerned about what goes on in England as the Englishman at home. Without putting too fine an edge on it, some of us don't like it when Britain is pushed around by those who should be seen off with a flea in the ear – or a gunboat! Or "accepting cheek" from those junior members of the Commonwealth "club" who should still be serving their apprenticeship in international relations. We don't like the thought that Britain might be going soft, although admittedly Mrs Thatcher is giving their come-uppance to the "wets". One worrying aspect, I would think, is the gradual erosion of the British heritage that I have observed over the years. I am sure that, in certain ears, "British heritage" is a discredited term, smacking of imperialism, racialism, elitism, jingoism and other expressions of disapproval that one finds in "progressive" circles. Progress is one thing but the wilful consigning to the dust heap of elements of what made Britain great is another.

Although I have been "putting it on" a bit in this last paragraph, it is this "Englishness" encountered in South Africa that can be misleading to the observer from afar. Listening to the South African Broadcasting Corporation, you might think from the voices that you are listening to the BBC, though with fewer egalitarian vowel sounds than encountered these days from London. What some people fail to realise is that South Africa is not British, some offshoot of the British Isles. It is to all intents and purposes a foreign country which, when you get down to basics, is more Third world than First, though the casual visitor will find this hard to appreciate when he enjoys all the civilised amenities he might expect. As one visitor who knows the African continent well remarked: "You've got to admit that things *work* in South Africa."

South Africa is an enormous country with a very wide diversity of races, cultures, colours, creeds and languages, and one thinks of the famous remark of General de Gaulle's about his own country: "How can you be expected to govern a country that has 246 kinds of cheese?" In short, South Africa's circumstances and its problems are unique and cannot be expected to parallel those of other countries.

3

You have no chance of understanding South Africa unless you understand what makes the Afrikaner "tick". I once tried to float the idea of a radio series under the title "The Unknown South African", with subtitle "the Afrikaner". This would have been directed at the local audience, but unfortunately I had no takers so the series was still-born. I chose that title "The Unknown South African" because in my view the Afrikaner is just that to many of his fellow South Africans (of whatever colour) and not least the English-speaker. Unless you appreciate the Afrikaner's background and motivation, you will have no chance of making sense of the South African situation.

The Afrikaner's origin is in a small party of Dutch settlers who landed with Commander Jan van Riebeeck in 1652 to establish a victualling station at the Cape of Good Hope for ships of the Dutch East India Company passing to and from Europe in the lucrative spice trade. This small community grew with the arrival of more settlers, including Huguenots who in 1688 fled to the Cape to escape religious persecution in France. Later, there were German settlers as well, all adding to the Afrikaner mix, and in 1820 the main wave of British settlers who gave an extra stir to the mix, although the assimilation in the early days was limited.

In 1795 and again in 1806, the English occupied the Cape by force. From 1836, those Dutch who were unhappy with English rule staged the Great Trek when some ten thousand men, women and children made the laborious and danger-ous journey by ox wagon into uncharted territory to find new homes to the north. They eventually settled in the Transvaal and the Orange Free State and in parts of Natal, having fought many fierce and savage battles against Black tribes and suffered massacre at their hands. It was then that some of the great names in the history of Afrikanerdom came to the fore . . . Andries Pretorius, Piet Retief, Hendrik Potgieter and others.

That perceptive writer H.V. Morton picked on this period in his book *In Search of South Africa*. He came out here immediately after World War II at the invitation of General Smuts and researched and wrote this book, subsequently making his home in South Africa not far from Cape Town. He broadcast on a number of occasions from the Cape Town studios, and this is the substance of one of his talks.

The events which led to the murder of Piet Retief and to the retribution that overtook Dingaan are the most dramatic in the true sense of the world in the history of this country. Quite a lot of history is not very interesting, like life itself, until it is illuminated by the struggle of the human spirit, and with such characters as Piet Retief, Dingaan and the avenging Pretorius, our story is lifted into the realm of the epic.

I am always struck by the fact, which I have never seen mentioned anywhere, that the Boer farmer might be called the originator of modern military methods. Waterloo was the last battle fought in the old military tradition, the professional army tradition, and all wars since then have been fought in khaki and field-grey, or in some other form of camouflage. The guerilla methods of Boer warfare have now become a specialised branch of military training all over the world, and even the word "commando" is firmly fixed in the modern textbook. I have also often thought that the farmers who rode out with the Bible in one hand and a flint-lock musket in the other bear a notable resemblance to Cromwell's Ironsides.

The Pilgrim Fathers of South Africa set out across the ocean of the veld and encountered the Zulu nation at the peak of its military proficiency. Their army was perhaps the most fearsome and efficient native fighting force seen in Africa since pharaonic times. Chaka, who succeeded Dinizwayo, was a Bantu Napoleon who had bequeathed to his successor Dingaan a perfectly trained and organised military machine. Inefficiency and cowardice were punished by instant death. The Zulu tactics were those of the modern pincer movement; the main body advanced to the attack, the reserve remained seated with its back to the fray until ordered to fling itself into battle.

The encounters of a few mounted farmers with this brave and terrible enemy have all the elements of Greek drama. The homespun cavalry become like characters in

5

Homer, they might be Greeks in corduroy. Fights such as Vegkop and Blood River read like Greek history. And, after all, were not Marathon and Thermopylae, which made such a stir in the world, merely small heroic encounters in the course of which a few resolved and devoted men pitted themselves against many? Potgieter with his elephant gun and his stabbed brother is like a figure out of Greek poetry, and so is Piet Retief going to his death over the Drakensberg, so is Pretorious riding like Nemesis to avenge his murder.

The point might well be made here that it wasn't only the Boers who fought the Black man. The British, during their occupation of the Cape, fought a series of so-called Kaffir wars on the eastern frontier, and in Natal there was the Zulu war, also with savage encounters. My own grandfather was killed at the disastrous battle of Isandhlwana in 1879 when a British force was surprised by a powerful Zulu impi and more than a thousand on the British side were wiped out. If anyone is minded to seek out file copies of the London *Daily Graphic*, my grandfather's portrait appears in the edition of 27th December 1879.

Continuing this very encapsulated history of the Afrikaner, then came two Anglo-Boer wars when, particularly in the second, the might of the British Empire was pitted against a small irregular army of farmers whose only professional cadre was an artillery unit. It is worth reading about this epic encounter of 1899/1902. It has been estimated that the Boer fighting force of some 60 000 never exceeded 25 000 men in the field at one time, whereas Britain, by the end of the struggle, had committed upwards of 400 000 British and Empire troops. A most comprehensive account is titled simply *The Boer War* by Thomas Pakenham, son of the distinguished historical biographer Elizabeth Longford; this was first published in 1979 by Weidenfeld and Nicolson. Another more recent publication is from Viking Penguin and is titled *To the Bitter End*, subtitled "a photographic history of the Boer War 1899–1902". The author is Emanoel Lee who is a consultant surgeon at the

John Radcliffe Hospital in Oxford, and he gives a wide-ranging account with illuminating statistics.

It might be noted here that, while there has been much talk in recent decades of wars of independence and liberation in Africa, nobody seems to have realised (or it has conveniently been forgotten) that the Boers were the first in Africa to challenge colonialism.

There were many foreign volunteers who served in the Anglo-Boer War. In the Uitlander Korps more than a dozen nationalities were represented, some of whom had served in armies in other places. Some of the names had interesting connections; for instance, Cor van Gogh, brother of the famous artist; Count Pecci, a nephew of Pope Leo XIII; Prince Louis d'Orléans et Braganza, cousin of the French pretender; Count von Zeppelin, a relative of the inventor.

A name that became famous was that of Sir Arthur Conan Doyle who served with the British Army as a medical officer and later created that famous detective of fiction, Sherlock Holmes. He had this to say in his book *The Great Boer War* (Bell, London 1900):

Take a community of Dutchmen of the type who defended themselves against all the power of Spain at the time when Spain was the greatest power in the world. Intermix them with a strain of those inflexible French Huguenots who gave up home and fortune and left their country at the time of the Edict of Nantes. The product must obviously be one of the most rugged, virile, unconquerable races ever seen upon the earth. Take this formidable people and train them for seven generations in constant warfare against savage men and ferocious beasts, in circumstances in which no weakling could survive; place them so that they acquire an exceptional skill with weapons and horsemanship, and give them a country which is eminently suitable to the tactics of the huntsman, the marksman and the rider. Then, finally put a fine temper upon their military qualities by a dour Old Testament religion and an ardent consuming patriotism. Combine all these qualities and all these impulses in one individual, and you have the modern Boer . . . the most

7

formidable antagonist who ever crossed the path of imperial Britain.

Some years ago I had the pleasure of interviewing for South African Television that "grand old man" of British politics, Labour peer Lord ("Mannie") Shinwell, who died in 1986 at the age of 101. He had been a lad in Glasgow when the second Anglo-Boer war broke out, and I remember him saying to me in the course of the interview "Worst thing Britain ever did was going to war against the Boers."

There was, of course, an appreciable though ineffective pro-Boer lobby in Britain at the time, but another aspect of moral support came from an unexpected source, an Australian war correspondent. Australians were among the Empire forces that fought against the Boers, and representing the *Sydney Morning Herald* and the Melbourne *Argus* was one A B Paterson, better known as "Banjo" Paterson, the so-called Australian bush poet. Earlier, he had written a ballad that was to make him famous – "Waltzing Matilda" that ranks with South Africa's "Sarie Marais" as akin to an unofficial national anthem.

In 1966, a biography of Paterson was published by the Australian firm of Angus and Robertson under the title *The Banjo of the Bush* in which the author, Clement Semmler, makes the point that, as the war progressed, Paterson's respect for "Johnny Boer" grew almost to admiration, and his anger at the propaganda used about and against the Boers prompted him to write with indignation and savage irony – a rare occurrence with the usually imperturbable and detached Paterson – his views concerning the war. As an example . . .

And first let us shriek the unstinted abuse that the Tory press prefer –
De Wet is a madam, and Steyn is a liar, and Kruger a pitiful cur!
(Though I think if Dom Paul – old as he is – were to walk down the Strand with his gun
A lot of these heroes would hide in the sewers or take to their heels and run! . . .)

Not the greatest poetry, but burningly sincere.

Bitter as was the struggle, it did have many manifestations of humanity. In fact, it has been referred to as "the last of the gentlemen's wars". The redoubtable General Koos de la Rey, one of the foremost of the Boer leaders, actually voted against the war in the Transvaal Volksraad, but seeing that it was inevitable, he personally conducted his children's English governess into Kimberley so that she could be with her own people.

H.V. Morton, in his book *In Search of South Africa* mentioned earlier, tells of the telegram that is preserved in the headmaster's study of St. Andrew's College in Grahamstown which at that time was in the British colony of the Cape of Good Hope. The telegram was sent by a father who served with the Boer forces and was despatched from Potchefstroom, in the South African Republic (Transvaal) on the eve of the outbreak of war. It read.

Leave for front tomorrow. Have wired twenty pounds your credit my son's school fees next quarter. Don't let him leave unless you have my signature for it. Further school fees will be safe. Best regards.

The Boer child remained at school in the British colony and when the war was over the backlog of fees was paid. H.V. Morton comments: "South Africa must be the only country in the world where you send your son to school with the enemy – and on tick"!

But might in the end triumphed, and this "army of farmers" as they were disparagingly referred to ("dammit man, they don't even wear uniform") went down to bitter defeat, with the two Boer republics of Transvaal and the Orange Free State devastated by the war. Apart from war casualties in the actual fighting, the Afrikaner had also suffered a terrible population loss through the death in the so-called concentration camps of an estimated 26 251 Boer women and children, of whom 22 000 were under the age of 16. In addition, a figure of 1 676 males over the age of 16, mostly elderly, is quoted as having died, as well as a substantial number of Blacks.

The concentration camps constitute one of the most

tragic episodes in South African history and attempts have been made to compare them with the German extermination camps of World War II. The comparison is entirely false. The British established concentration camps (literally to concentrate the rural population) as part of the strategy to deny the roving Boer commandos a source of supply and support, and also to move the women and children to where they could be safe from possible attack by bands of marauding Black tribesmen. But the British administration, certainly in the early days, was not equipped to handle such numbers and conditions became very bad in many instances, with deaths mounting steadily. Along with the forced removals to the concentration camps went the burning of farms which also left a legacy of bitterness.

After the war, English-isation continued apace, and economic power resulting from the discovery of gold on the Witwatersrand in 1886 was firmly in the hands of "the enemy". The Afrikaner had lost his country.

Also, there were the affronts offered to him, unwitting as some of them may have been. As far back as 1878, the famous English novelist Anthony (*Barchester Towers*) Trollope came to South Africa and wrote a two-volume report on his experiences and impressions. About Bloemfontein, capital of the Orange Free State Republic, he wrote:

We first repudiate the country and then we take upon ourselves to appoint a high church dignitary whom we send out from England with a large accompaniment of minor ecclesiastics. In the United States they have bishops of the Protestant Episcopal Church as well as of the Roman Catholic Church. But they are not bishops of the Church of England. Here in Bloemfontein the Church is English, and prays for the Queen before the President – for which latter it sometimes does pray and sometimes does not. I attended the Cathedral service twice and such was my experience. This is strange for an Englishman who visits the Republic prepared to find it a nationality of itself . . . I am very far from finding fault. The Church in Bloemfontein has worked very well and has done much good. But in acknowledging this, I think we ought to acknowledge also that very much is due to the forbearance of the Boers.

(*South Africa* by Anthony Trollope, published by Chapman Hall, London 1879)

1910, when the Transvaal and the Orange Free State joined with the Cape and Natal to form the Union of South Africa, saw little improvement in the Afrikaner's lot, and he even found forces at work to abolish his language. He was very much a second-class citizen. The Afrikaner had traditionally been a rural dweller ("Boer" actually means farmer) and up to that time his role in the professions had been limited. Commerce and industry, such as there was, was almost exclusively in other hands, and the Afrikaner had to pull himself up by his own bootstraps to achieve the position he enjoys today. The transition from rural to urban dweller can be traumatic, as any sociologist will tell you, and the poor-white problem that haunted him for decades is not far back in the Afrikaner's memory. Recently, a Black South African, Mr P G Gumede, vice-president of the National African Federated Chamber of Commerce (NAFCOC) referred to this period in addressing businessmen in Britain. He said: "It is important to study the history of the Afrikaner to understand the South African situation – especially since the South African (Anglo-Boer) war, which left the Afrikaner poorer and more scorned than most Black people today".

But it is worth recording in this context the acknowledgment made by the South African Minister of Finance, Barend du Plessis, to the effect that it had been the English-speaking taxpayer who, over the years, had subsidised the development of the Afrikaner.

Summing it up, it is not surprising that the Afrikaner displays certain sensitivities. Having struggled over many decades to get where he is, and having had experience of his country being attacked and taken away from him, is it any wonder that he does not take easily to the idea that this could happen again . . . different scenario and different cast, but same result?

11

ONE MAN ONE VOTE

Democracy means simply the bludgeoning of the people
by the people for the people.   *(Oscar Wilde)*

This is the great parrot-cry of the age . . . one man one vote
(in a unitary state). The expectation is that it will bring
about "democracy" on the Westminster model. Its advocates seldom pause to think that there might be alternatives
better suited to satisfactory government, depending on the
individual circumstances, and that the Westminster system
is not necessarily suited to every circumstance; as has so
often been said, the Westminster system was never intended
for export.

   In the 1970's, when I was in Europe recording programmes for the South African Broadcasting Corporation, I
sought out the noted Spanish historian and former dip-
lomat, Salvador de Madariaga. He was living at Ascona,
looking out over Lake Maggiore, having come there from
Oxford where he had had a long university association. I
recorded a wide-ranging conversation with him and I kept
the transcript of portion of it that has a bearing on this
question of democracy.

   This is what he said:

   I happen to be far more interested in liberty than in
democracy. I think liberty is an essential thing of our
civilisation; democracy is pure machinery. And the concentration of all the West – led, I believe, by one of the
sorriest brands of intellectuals that the West has ever suffered – is on democracy . . . and democracy is only worth
whatever the amount of liberty it conveys and can ensure.
And I see now, as one of the greatest triumphs of the
enemies of liberty, that no-one speaks of liberty and
everyone speaks of democracy.

12

The world had a period when it was led by the aristocracy; it wasn't badly led. And then there came the control of the nation by the bourgeoisie, by the middle class. It is now the fashion, even among the intellectuals of the bourgeoisie who are themselves bourgeois, to throw stones at it. But it is absolutely obvious that 90 per cent of the achievements of science, art, progress, cleanliness, amenities and everything, is due to the bourgeoisie during the last two centuries or three. And then now has come, owing to the working of universal suffrage, the kingdom of the majority.

Now the majority are not by nature able to produce the capacity, the intellectual capacity, of either the bourgeoisie or the aristocracy. You see, there is, I think, in the world today a formidable error which is to imagine that a nation is composed of the sum total of its citizens, and if the citizens split into two, and 50 percent – or say 51 per cent – are of one opinion, and 49 per cent are of the other opinion, by definition the first, the 51 per cent, are right and the 49 per cent are wrong.

Well, all that seems to me completely idiotic, and my definition of a nation is entirely different. A nation is not the sum total of its individuals; a nation is the integration of its institutions, and what we want to hear about is what do the institutions of the nation think, and not what the sum total of a Mr Smith, Mr Jones and Tom, Dick and Harry think, because that has no interest whatsoever.

I might just say that, in our normal elastic terms of reference, Salvador de Madariaga – with his background – would doubtless be classified as a "liberal", although the liberal cry throughout the world tends to be unqualified "one man one vote in a unitary state". However, for us South Africans there is the distressing example in other parts of our continent where one-man-one-vote has in effect been "one-man-one-vote . . . once", leading to a one-party dictatorship.

Coincidentally, about the same time as I had the privilege of interviewing Salvador de Madariaga, I had the chance of meeting the eminent British historian Arnold Toynbee. I sought him out in Yorkshire, where he was living in retirement and made a long recording with him for a series of programmes under the title "Britain Today".

This is an extract:

The British till now – the last few centuries – rather successfully combined a great deal of liberty with a respect for authority. So did the Americans originally. The founding fathers of the United States were aristocrats, really, and the mass of the people were content to follow their lead. But in all the parliamentary countries now people aren't willing to follow the lead of people who have greater ability, a greater understanding of the nation. This is very dangerous not only for democracy but for the existence of nations. I don't think all people are equal. We all have certain fundamental rights that are equal, but our ability, and our power to contribute to society, is not equal, and this fact of nature ought to be recognised.

By coincidence, while I was preparing this manuscript, a question was submitted to a radio quiz for which I am responsible. The questioner asked:

Who said "Democracy means giving equal voting rights to people having unequal ability to think"?

The answer submitted by this listener (which she took from the book *Charles and Diana* by Ralph G Martin, Grafton Books, 1986) was "Prince Charles, now Prince of Wales, in an essay he wrote at the age of 16 at Gordonstoun School."

In considering the South African situation, something else that is worth bearing in mind was said by Brian Crozier, at the time Director-General of the Institute for the Study of Conflict in London, in his book *The Minimum State* published by Hamish Hamilton in 1979:

It is not the least of the structural absurdities of the party system that it paves the way for the enemies of democracy.

All of the foregoing suggests clearly that Westminster-style democracy is not Holy Writ. Those who lock their minds to the idea that there might be systems better suited to individual circumstances could be considered as being either ingenuous or having a very specific axe to grind.

With the progressive dismantling of apartheid, South Africa is exploring various constitutional options in order to do justice to its many different communities. I stress "different" because critics abroad all too often regard the South African situation simplistically as a Black versus White struggle. This is to ignore completely the make-up of the South African population.

Some time ago, when I was responsible for a weekly radio book review programme, an American publisher on his first visit to South Africa called on me to discuss book matters. We then went on to general topics including social and political matters, and he told me that he found it interesting to compare the reality with the image of South Africa that he had gained from media reports in his own country. I gave him some figures that gave him pause to ponder. I said to him "If you had in your country (the United States of America) the population proportions that we have in our country (South Africa), you would have a very interesting situation. Leaving small minorities out of the calculation, and basing the argument on round figures, and putting your population (very roughly, for the sake of argument) at 200 million Whites and 25 million Blacks, if you had the population proportions we have in South Africa, you would have no fewer than a billion Blacks (using American terminology viz 1 000 000 000). What is more, yours would not be a homogeneous Black population but one split into any number of nations or tribes, nor would there necessarily be great amity between them." I made this final point: "A billion Blacks might alter some perceptions in your country." This American looked at me for several seconds, and then he said with a rather wry smile "I guess so."

Americans generally speaking could have the grace to acknowledge that, compared with the immensely complicated historical and ethnic situation presented in South Africa, they took an unconscionably long time to come to grips with their racial "problems" – and have not yet solved

15

them, bar granting the vote in a unitary state. But when you are granting the vote to a minority, that is perfectly safe. If however, as I implied in the previous paragraph, the United States of America had had the same population proportions as we have in South Africa, which would have meant a *thousand million American Blacks* to, say, two hundred million Whites, what then? Would the Whites not have felt that they risked a total ceding of power?

Various ploys are adopted to "show solidarity" with the South African Blacks, such as picketing the South African embassy in Washington DC. But this was easily recognised as a transparent manoeuvre to gain a bit of mileage when Black causes in the United States tended to be at a low ebb . . . and it provided political, and even showbiz, personalities with not unwelcome publicity. But where was the show of solidarity with, say, the Blacks of Uganda when Idi Amin was applauded by other African heads of state when he walked into a summit wearing his Stetson and six-shooters, having just presided over the massacre of several thousand Ugandans, including the Anglican Archbishop? The world at large could do with less of this selective indignation, and those who have any respect for rational thinking, and their own intellectual integrity, would do well to eschew it.

Although South Africa is a combination of a First-world and a Third-world country (with the latter aspect predominating), it is certainly part of the Western world. Its population proportions and its racial, ethnic and cultural diversity make a nonsense of the glib demands made of it. When it comes to the much-peddled word "integration", why should it be assumed that every component of our complex population would be happy to integrate with others? How much success would be achieved in integrating, say, the Balkan countries with their strong nationalistic and cultural differences? One does not have to be white to be concerned who one's neighbours are. If a South African Asian does not want to "assimilate" with a Black South African, it is not necessarily so much a question of colour as radical cultural difference.

What about the troubles in Fiji between the indigenous islanders and the Indian section of the population? In Cyprus, are the Greeks and Turks after all these years going to be persuaded into playing "happy families"?

In similar circumstances of racial, cultural or religious disharmony, there has at times been a flimsy form of unity against the "oppressor", but take that away and the dogs are at one another's throats.

Having just used the expression "the dogs are at one another's throats", I have to remind myself of the sensitivities that can be aroused even in the use of metaphor. British Airways is obviously an organisation that knows something about sensitivies. Reading my copy of their in-flight magazine *High Life*, I came upon a note in the map section: "These maps are for the convenience of passengers and have no political significance".

Or what about the talk by that superb broadcaster Alistair Cooke in which he told of the policy adopted by a well-known New York progressive school in which 90 per cent of the pupils are Jewish. When it came to cast the end-of-term play (which was *The Merchant of Venice*), every member of the cast was Jewish – except one, Shylock. *His* real name was Cynthia Adams.

But seriously, when it comes to integration, the disputed Group Areas Act here in South Africa is a very thorny problem and has caused, and is still causing, a lot of unhappiness. More of this in a later chapter.

It was ironic to read a report in our newspapers in February 1985 headlined "Integration not the solution – Black activist". It concerned James Meredith, the Black American who made history with his pioneering fight for Black civil rights. In 1962, as many people will remember, his demands to be enrolled as a student at the all-white University of Mississippi sparked race riots that forced President Kennedy to send thousands of Federal troops to the state to keep order. Mr Meredith was reported as now campaigning against integration, saying that integration has made Blacks worse off than at any time in history, including the period of slavery. To what extent that view is shared by other Blacks is not provable, of course, but during two visits to the United States in the 1970's I had a number of comments from Blacks about the degree of discrimination that still existed. One hopes that it has declined in the intervening years, but how odd that virtually on the day (if not the very day) that the United States legislators overrode President Reagan's veto on sanctions against South Africa because of its "discriminatory policies", a report was released in the United States on racial discrimination in housing in the Washington DC area. Also, according to a report, the 700 000 inhabitants of the American capital, three quarters of whom are Black, have no constitutional voting rights – only a token representation.

In 1985, there was a report from New Zealand of a Maori professor at the University of Wellington, himself a Maori Council delegate, who told a seminar in Parliament that the country's one-man-one-vote system of democracy is unfair as it gives the Whites a ten-to-one advantage over the Maoris. It would be illuminating for anyone abroad to consider that argument in relation to the population proportions in South Africa (see end of chapter).

In Australia, things are not necessarily all rosy. In March 1986, a report of the Aboriginal Affairs Minister warned that racial tension was high in various parts of Australia, and even the Pope, on his visit in November 1986, sharply chided Australians for their treatment of the Aborigines.

There was an ironically hilarious incident in Canada in March 1987, but one with serious undertones, in the visit by the South African Ambassador in Ottawa to a Red Indian reserve north of Winnipeg. This was as a result of a magazine article by the Ambassador on what he called "Canada's blindspots". This brought an invitation from the Chief of the Peguis people for the Ambassador to visit his remote reserve, his aim being to highlight the conditions and plight of his people as he felt his government was ignoring them. He succeeded beyond expectation because some

80 TV and press reporters and photographers traipsed across the barren, snow-covered stretches of prairie in what was undeniably a publicity coup for the Chief. It was highly embarassing for the Canadian government because only the month before, the Canadian Prime Minister had been in southern Africa playing footsie with Black leaders over the iniquities of South Africa. The South African Ambassador's reaction was confined to a diplomatic comment: "Canada should sweep in front of its own house before telling anybody to do so in front of theirs".

An equally amusing sequel to this incident was the reported intention of the Chief to seek foreign aid from Pretoria! Although I don't particularly like playing *tu quoque* with critics, I must mention a further irony that emerged from a report prepared for Canada's External Affairs Department. It stated that the Canadian Embassy in Pretoria had "considerable scope for improvement" in employment terms for Blacks, and that it had fallen short of its own standards by which Canadian businesses are judged.

When one thinks of all the glib solutions to South Africa's problems that are offered from abroad, it is salutary to remember the words attributed to Winston Churchill: "In countries where there is only one race, broad and lofty views are taken of the colour question." To this one might add: "In countries where the Whites are in the great majority, they can afford to be 'liberal'."

As a further bar to understanding is the fact that in various parts of the world where race dominance exists, it has lasted so long and become so mixed up with fate and destiny as not to be regarded as racial at all. Furthermore, a sentimental view is taken of certain countries because these countries are judged to be "romantic", ignoring aspects of inequality or poverty or violence. A British travel writer has remarked about the famous (and romantic) Golden Temple in Amritsar, a stronghold of the Sikhs, that it is "surrounded by some of the meanest streets and most dreadful human squalor imaginable". Can some of the Sikh brutalities, or the continuing Hindu/Moslem atrocities, be more easily overlooked because India and Pakistan are considered to be "romantic" countries? Can some of the long-established discrimination be condoned because it has been going on for so long? The untouchables might have a word to add here.

The assumption exists in certain quarters abroad that South Africa has a homogeneous Black population, which is certainly not the case as figures at the end of this chapter will make clear. If it were so, we would not have the incidence of faction fights when members of one tribe or national group brutally slaughter members of another. Unlike Britain and the United States, where the Black section of the population has had considerable exposure to a Western way of life, the process as far as the bulk of the South African Black population is concerned has been much slower. Many are still emerging from a tribal society while many remain in a tribal state. I say this is no disparagement (I sometimes wonder whether it is not a happier state than the complications of Western civilisation!) but merely to try to point out a more realistic perspective within which to view the evolving South African situation. Let it not be assumed that one can put evolution into a microwave oven to hurry up the process.

I write as a White African. I am not a colonial, and this continent is my home. I am the first to recognise the frustrations suffered by many of our Black people and I pay tribute to those many who are patiently and steadily working their way up the economic and social ladder and who consider that, at this stage, a job is more important than the vote. (You don't have to be Black to appreciate that!) We have in the Black community any number of men and women of distinction, achievement and humanity whose success is all the more laudable in an unequal society – of which South Africa is not the only example.

Here one must take into account the political frustration suffered by the more educated and emancipated Black. He had most probably lost his tribal allegiances and did not see his future, political or otherwise, in some "own area" but rather in the established (White) cities. It is difficult not to have sympathy with these frustrations which, whether or not fomented by agitators, have led to periodic unrest over the decades, resulting in the present situation in which South Africa finds itself arraigned before the world. Again, however much one may deplore the violence with which the African National Congress (ANC) is now associated, it should be remembered that it came into being a long time ago as a peaceable political organisation that found its aims and ambitions increasingly blocked – and this started well before the present Nationalist government came into power.

But, at this stage, despite what has happened in the past and amid all the constitutional discussion and jockeying for position, all parties concerned with the future of South Africa will have to accept that negotiation and compromise are the watchwords and that the "winner takes all" political philosophy promoted by the Westminster concept is just "not on".

It is vital to an understanding of the South African situation to appreciate that it does not have a homogeneous population but is a complex amalgam of minorities whose rights have to be protected by negotiation.

This extract from a report appeared in a newspaper in the early part of 1986:

> Black people's grievances are many. The extent of social deprivation and racial disadvantages makes life intolerable. Harsh policing on top of all this provides the chemistry for violent reaction.

That was not referring to South Africa but was taken from a report sponsored by the West Midland County Council on the previous year's riots in Handsworth, Birmingham. If this is considered to be an exaggeration and an unfair comment on the situation in Britain, who is to say that perceptions abroad of the South African situation are not also exaggerated? I am not in any sense suggesting that all is well in my country, but the question of perspective enters the picture again.

It is significant that an opinion poll conducted in South Africa in the first part of 1986 (when there was a high level of unrest in the townships) showed that 75,4 per cent of

21

Blacks believed that nothing was being gained out of the unrest situation. There are many responsible Blacks who deplore the violence, the senseless burning down of amenities that have been built for the Black communities, the destruction of vital educational facilities, the burning of school books with the slogan "freedom before education". The responsible members of the community realise that there is a grave danger of creating an entire "lost generation" of unemployables. Even Black youth organisations expressed concern at the escalation of Black-on-Black violence and the harassing of innocent people. The so-called "necklace killings", where the victim has a tyre put round his neck, soaked in petrol and then set alight, shocks the senses, particularly as youngsters are responsible for many of these incidents. The South African Police have the thankless – and dangerous – task of trying to keep the peace and to protect moderate and law-abiding Blacks from extremists and criminals. Such is the corruption of the "liberation vocabulary" that these acts are considered to be justifiable violence "against the system" and not just plain murder as they certainly are.

In this context, Mrs Winnie Mandela has been quoted as saying "With our boxes of matches and our'necklaces' we shall liberate this country." ANC leader Oliver Tambo was quoted by the *New York Times* as saying "When blacks learn that a white has died in the violence that has become a common feature of the South African political situation, that kind of thing comes like a drop of rain after a long drought." The *Wall Street Journal* adds another Tambo statement "The killing of white civilians would have the beneficial effect of getting white people used to bleeding."

Mr Tambo is still being invited around the world to "spread the message", a recent invitation being from the Prime Minister of Australia, Mr Bob Hawke. From reports, it appears that some of the more clear thinking Australians did not give Mr Tambo a smooth ride, indicating that not everybody in the West is being duped by double talk.

Nobody should be under any illusions as to the strategy being played out. It has been deployed in other parts of the world – in Vietnam, for instance. Kill your responsible and moderate leaders, as well as "collaborators" such as policemen and others, intimidate the mass of the population, and generally make the society ungovernable and so prepare the way for the overthrow of the existing regime and its replacement by a Marxist autocracy.

The ANC has assumed a high profile among world opinion formers, and it is hardly necessary to wonder who foots the bill for their expensive public relations exercises, the cost of establishing offices, the unlimited trips undertaken by their upper echelon, and the arms and ammunition and explosives used against mainly "soft" targets in South Africa. The fact is that a high proportion of the ANC's executive are members of the South African Communist Party. In the face of this, it strikes one as odd that Dr Mangosuthu Buthelezi, political head of the Zulu nation (the largest Black group in South Africa) tends to be written off as a "stooge", even by those who should not lend themselves to such deceit, as he is against violence.

The improvements that continue to be made in the standard of living of the Black communities in South Africa must necessarily be viewed against the daunting numbers and the disproportionate growth of the Black population, and viewed within the limits of available finances. In the overall African context, it can well be asked whether the emphasis should now be placed not on political rights but on Africa's population explosion and its growing inability to feed itself. This may be an inheritance from the San Francisco Conference in 1945 to establish the United Nations when the emphasis was on power and politics. The basic problem of the masses of mankind – getting enough to eat – was given short shrift. It is pertinent here to quote Jonathan Swift's wise words from *Gulliver's Travels*:

> And he gave it for his opinion, that whoever could make two ears of corn or two blades of grass to grow upon a spot of ground where only one grew before, would deserve better of mankind, and do more essential service

23

to his country than the whole race of politicians put together.

The development of agriculture is only one exciting story in South Africa – the enormous amount of money and effort that has been put to helping the Black population develop as agriculturists from a largely pastoral background. The success stories here are legion. As just one example, a rice growing industry has been developed in the self-governing state of KaNgwane and in northern Natal, and the quality of the product has brought commendation from Chinese experts.

Great emphasis is placed these days on human rights but little is said about human obligations. One does not need to be a prophet to forecast that the future of the African continent will be tied up with its ability to feed an exploding population. Alarming figures have been published, and, to take only one aspect as far as South Africa is concerned, the average age of our population (all races) is 17, which means that the younger mass of the population has to be supported by the older population. With more than six million Black children at school in our country, the drain on resources needs no over-stating. It has been estimated that the South African population will multiply almost five times over the next six decades. At the present time, the Whites are out-numbered almost 5–1 by the Blacks, and the ratio is expected to rise to around 17–1 by the year 2040.

According to the Chief Executive of the Associated Chambers of Commerce of South Africa, if South Africa's Black population continued to grow at its present rate, all efforts to promote economic growth would be neutralised. If South Africa were fortunate enough to realise a 3,5 per cent growth rate in its gross domestic product, almost two-thirds of it would be swallowed up by the additional mouths that would have to be fed. "The Black population stands to lose the most if this happens", he said. Fortunately, there are indications now that the birth rate, certainly as far as the urban Black population is concerned, is falling as a direct corollary of a rise in their economic situation.

So the unprejudiced observer of the South African scene might sympathise if we were to flash a sign as is sometimes done on television: "We have a problem; please be patient." I remember years ago a colleague of mine went along to an anti-apartheid rally in London to see what went on. When prayers were offered for the Blacks of South Africa, this man suggested that prayers be offered also for the Whites of South Africa, that they be given guidance in the making of some uniquely weighty decisions.

But manipulation of public opinion is a big industry these days. A 1986 opinion poll in Britain had a question phrased "Are you more sympathetic to the Black people of South Africa, or the White government?" The answers must have been a foregone conclusion.

POPULATION OF SOUTH AFRICA: 1985 ESTIMATE

Whites	4 900 000
Coloured	2 800 000
Asian	861 000
Black	19 000 000
among whom the numerically most important are	
Zulu	6 400 000
Xhosa	2 900 000
North Sotho	2 900 000
South Sotho	1 900 000
Tswana	1 400 000
Shangaan/Tsonga	1 100 000
Swazi	1 000 000
South Ndebele	428 000
North Ndebele	290 000
Venda	209 000
Total population of South Africa (estimated)	27 700 000

THAT ALBATROSS WORD

If apartheid didn't exist, it would have to be invented.

The story has been around for a long time of the immigrant who has been in South Africa for a year or so. Asked how he finds it, he replies: "Everything's fine, we like it here." He goes on to say that he has a good job, they have a house and a car, the kids are happy at school, and they are even saving to buy his wife a car. "But" he says, "there are two things I don't like about South Africa. One is apartheid, and the other is all these blacks around the streets." Apocryphal, but could be true.

The point needs to be made that the Afrikaner did not invent apartheid (separateness). Some of the Dutch who are so uptight about South Africa's policies should realise that it was their settlers at the Cape of Good Hope in 1652 who were the first to practise a discriminatory approach in a multi-racial situation, and this continued through the British colonial period in South Africa. What the Nationalist Afrikaner did was to use the word as a compelling electioneering slogan in 1948 and to entrench the policy in legislation. Then they surrounded it with an awesome number of regulations and established a vast bureaucracy to administer it. The size of this bureaucracy (taking into account the many fringe benefits and the "cradle to grave" coddling that public servants enjoy) has been a serious drain on the South African economy and accounts to some extent for the problems facing the country at the present time.

Apartheid has become such a bogy word throughout the world that the point must be stressed that it has no sinister built-in meaning. In Afrikaans it means simply separateness. Although apartheid is discriminatory, it was not conceived as discrimination *against* the non-White. Nor was it based on alleged inferiority so much as a recognition of difference. It is important to realise that *equality* with the Whites, but in separate areas, was the keystone of the policy. The fact that it has not been fully achieved does not invalidate the point.

So, South Africa had a government from 1948 that was going to clean up the mess (as they saw it) left by their predecessors and organise once and for all the future of race relationships in our country. Although a little far-fetched, there is a smidgeon of comparison with another attempt to legislate for the rest of time – Hitler's 1000-year Reich . . . and look what happened to him! Actually, the rather laissez-faire approach of previous governments (the "mess" referred to earlier) would probably have seen the continuing evolution of a stratified South African society practising a form of social and economic apartheid as is found in other parts of the world. There would still have been inequities, as in all other parts of the world, but South Africa would not have had a policy that has been branded as insensitive, arrogant and inhuman. This was certainly not the intention; it was not an unrelenting attrition against the non-white. Individuals were affected to a greater or lesser degree; for the tribal African it was very much a case of "business as usual". Despite everything, a remarkable degree of goodwill persisted between the races, and there were many individuals and organisations working to ameliorate conditions for those most affected. In such a regimented system, however, their efforts were not always successful.

There is one aspect of apartheid that is almost invariably ignored and that is the important one of decentralisation (into the homelands or, as they were disparagingly referred to, the Bantustans). The policy of spreading population and industrial and commercial activity and water utilisation more evenly throughout a country has commended itself to governments in other parts of the world, but its application in South Africa has been condemned. Certainly it has not worked out as fully as had been hoped, but the policy had theoretical logic behind it in aiming to provide equal opportunities and amenities – and political rights – in the respective Black states. A plus factor which is seldom taken into account is the fact that the implementation of the policy (into which a great deal of money has been poured, mostly from White pockets) has provided training and managerial and entrepreneurial experience to a large number of Blacks. The subsequent granting of self-government (and later, in some cases, independence) to a number of Black national states has added political experience. Under a policy of laissez-faire, "God help the hindmost" and all that, the process would have been much slower.

It remains an odd quirk of international attitudes that the independence of the four states originally within South Africa (Transkei, Bophuthatswana, Venda and Ciskei) is not recognised, one reason being that they receive grants from South Africa and are therefore "not truly independent". But what about the independent states to the north which receive large injections of foreign aid? What is the difference? Also, the world community would seem to deny the people of those four countries a pride in nationhood. Bophuthatswana is bigger than any number of independent nations throughout the world that have membership of the United Nations. For example, it is bigger than Belgium, Denmark or the Netherlands, let alone countries like Israel, Lesotho (which lies within the borders of South Africa), Lebanon, El Salvador, Gambia, Iceland, Fiji, Malta, Tonga and others.

There is another argument put forward in this context and that is the desirability of communities evolving as a cohesive unit, with the emancipated helping – not least by example – to develop those who are still climbing the evolutionary ladder. Some sociologists will agree that if you hive off the better-educated and generally more advanced section, you abandon the mass of the community to a much slower rate of development. I am not pushing this argument, because the Group Areas Act has had the effect in many instances of uprooting settled non-White communities and casting them into unattractive residential areas, often far from their places of employment. The complaint heard from the upper class among these communities has been "Why do we have to be thrown cheek by jowl with slum dwellers?". This argument is hard to refute. Admittedly, over the years, these new non-White areas have improved to some extent, there has been a gradual shaking down and stratification of the society, but it has been a slow process and the attrition and unhappiness has been enormous – and sad-making to many of us.

For anyone to argue "How would the Whites like it if these same slum-dwellers were to move in with them?" does not really hold water. Economic factors such as property prices would bring about an automatic "apartheid", but this applies more to the economically advanced section of the White population. When it comes to the working class White, the situation is very different; he finds himself to an extent competing with the non-White in employment and housing areas, and this is the breeding ground for racial intolerance and racial "incidents". Here I would like to suggest that anyone abroad reading this does not indulge in an easy "holier than thou" attitude; this same overseas reader, whether in Britain, Europe, America or elsewhere won't have far to look to find similar examples of racial attitudes. For instance, in May 1987 the Executive Director of the National Association for the Advancement of Coloured People in the United States was quoted as saying "We have more hatred now because we have entered a new era, an era of competition for jobs, attention and power."

I want to interpolate an experience I had in the early 1950's which has a bearing on the question of separate development. I went on assignment to the Transkei (this was before it became the independent state of Transkei) to do a radio feature about the territory. One of my visits was to the agricultural college established by the South African government at Tsolo, some little distance from Umtata, the capital, for the purpose of training Transkeian Blacks in all agricultural processes. With a growing population it was becoming more and more necessary for the people to be able to feed themselves.

29

The most fascinating aspect of my visit was to see the demonstration small-holding that had been specially laid out and equipped. The total extent was about six acres, of which one acre was divided into four to accommodate living quarters, cow byre and storage, vegetable plot, and pens and runs for poultry. The other five or so acres would be devoted to maize. I was told that a family could establish themselves on a self-build basis at very low cost and thereafter would be self sufficient and also income-earning from surplus maize that they would market. It seemed to me to be the absolute answer in a Third-world environment, but I came upon unexpected snags. The first was that of the three agricultural colleges that had existed in the Transkei, Tsolo was the only one remaining, the other two having been closed because of lack of applicants. The second was that, while the college offered a two-year diploma course after which the student was qualified as an agricultural demonstrator and could walk straight into a well-paid job (such was the need for improved agricultural methods in the Transkei), a distressing number of students gaining their diploma preferred to go to Johannesburg and get jobs as tea "boys" in offices.

Deplorable as this may be in respect of a government's desire to offer developmental opportunities to Black South Africans, it is to some extent understandable; the drift to the cities is a world-wide phenomenon. It shows itself in South Africa, also, in the disproportion between Black doctors practising in the urban areas and those practising in the rural areas; there is the inevitable and understandable attraction of the "bright lights". The result is that the gaps in rural medicine in Black areas have had to be filled by White doctors.

As sociologists well know, the drift to the cities (all too often it is a rush) can have the most dire social consequences. South Africa has its Crossroads which has become a focus for world criticism, but there are Crossroads equivalents in other parts of the world, and to believe otherwise, or not to accept the fact, is a sign either of naïveté or gross sophistry. In short, the whipped-up emotion surrounding

Crossroads lacks balance and perspective. This is not to deny that there has been much to deplore about Crossroads, nor that the authorities have been guilty of insensitive handling of the problem, but, with a huge unprogrammed influx, a solution to the problem could not be found overnight. Ironically, this influx was a direct result of the lifting of influx control, one of the steps in the government's easing of apartheid. However, a process of upgrading of the Crossroads area has been going on. It is soon to achieve local authority status, and the thousands of refugees rendered homeless by the fighting between Black factions there, who have not already been accommodated in Khayelitsha, will be able to return. Khayelitsha (a Xhosa word meaning 'new home') is a big replacement township growing up rapidly a few kilometres down the main road between Cape Town and Somerset West, more about which later in this chapter. But back to the subject of apartheid.

As the world should know but is reluctant to acknowledge, the apartheid policy is being dismantled . . . and again the world is reluctant to recognise the comparative speed with which this is being done. That is why I have had to update this manuscript a number of times. A good proportion of world opinion calls for an "instant fix" . . . one-man-one-vote in a unitary state and hey presto, Utopia. But will anybody bet that Black majority rule would bring about the economic millennium for all sections of the population, or, for that matter, that there would be "democracy", as we know it? Examples in other parts of Africa do not inspire much confidence.

Some years ago, a distinguished South African (a "liberal" in the terminology of the time) Dr. Ellen Hellmann made this comment.

If these decades of rapid social change have demonstrated anything, it is surely that "solutions" to human problems are not found; at best, mankind can hope to find acceptable processes leading to acceptable goals.

That is why the South African government, albeit very late in the day, is exploring constitutional options to achieve these "acceptable goals". But the world wants a "quick fix" and threatens stepped-up sanctions.

In 1976, when I was in the United States recording radio programmes reflecting the American bicentenary, I had a long conversation in New York with Leo Rosten. I remember him showing me with some pride the grapevine growing on the balcony of his 19th floor apartment over-looking the seething traffic of Manhattan. Leo Rosten is the author of a diversity of books, including that humorous near-classic *The Education of H*Y*M*A*N K*A*P*L*A*N* writ-ten under the pseudonym Leonard Q Ross. He is also a political and social scientist and commentator and we were talking about reform in the context of the civil rights cam-paign in the United States and some of its more question-able manifestations. These are his words.

> The basic trouble with the reformer is that he suggests those things which, if done, will make him feel better. Now that hasn't anything to do with what the objective consequences of that will be. Not long ago I gave an address in which I said the trouble with some good and well-intentioned reformers is that it never occurs to them how much worse things can be made. Now this is not to discourage idealism by any manner or means, and I'm sure I'm considered a reformer by many people whom I consider rigid or unrealistic. I want to reform a great many things, but I hope that I make myself think through the consequences of such reforms. For instance, human behaviour is not to be dismissed simply because aspects of it are not liked by you or me . . .

In this context, without wishing to sound facetious, it has historically been noted that, with the rise of Christianity, the church banned public baths, and for centuries in the Middle Ages people stank.

I must make the point that I am not using Leo Rosten to support a South African point of view, but merely quoting something that is of universal application. Pascal put it this way: "The first principle of morality is thinking clearly."

What Leo Rosten said in that first paragraph about the reformer suggesting those things that will make him feel better, irrespective of the consequences, falls fairly and squarely alongside stereotyped perceptions of South Africa from abroad.

"Feelgoodie" is the word to apply to such people. I wish I knew who invented it because I would like to pay him or her handsome credit for putting a finger on one of the great hypocrisies of the age . . . as long as you feel good, as long as you've joined the pack, it doesn't matter a damn whether or not you know anything about the subject; you're going to express the popular line of disapproval because it makes you feel good . . . you're a feelgoodie. Put more crudely, you're a moral masturbator.

Examples of the breed proliferate, and here are only a few:

Politicians and officials from abroad who come grand-standing to impress an electorate back home, particularly if there is a Black vote to be courted. If you are running for office, or think that you might do so in the future, then you have to watch out. Many of these people have an axe to grind that one suspects might bear little relation to the real welfare of the Blacks of South Africa. They seek out emotive situations previously identified by other ideologues. One newspaper called this "compassioneering". These visitors are recognised by the short duration of their stay and the highly selective list of people to whom they speak. As with certain fact-finding (so-called) missions, they signal the message "My mind is made up, don't confuse me with facts." These are maxi-feelgoodies. Odd as it may sound, they don't fool all South African Blacks, many of whom resent their visits.

Another example of the feelgoodie brotherhood is those countries that blackmailed the Stoke Mandeville Games Federation into banning the South African team of disabled sportsmen and sportswomen from the 1985 Games. This was a non-racial team representing all population groups. Here was a case of exploitation of the disabled for political ends, overriding the fact that these people are excluded from the normal world of sport. Cruel, craven and cynical as it was, the action undoubtedly produced its crop of feel-goodies.

There was a more recent instance when the South African team was barred from the International Transplant Games in Austria. The team was already in Innsbruck when the Austrian government, which owns all the sports facilities used for the Games, stepped in and imposed a ban. An Austrian newspaper described in a front-page article how a Black child sat in the grandstand with tears streaming down his face as he watched the games in which he should have been competing.

Aldous Huxley put it rather well:

The surest way to work up a crusade in favour of some good cause is to promise people that they will have a chance of maltreating someone. To be able to destroy with good conscience, to be able to behave badly and call your bad behaviour "righteous indignation", this is the height of psychological luxury, the most delicious of moral treats.

In other instances, Black athletes who have no problem competing in South Africa where sport is non-racial have been banned from competing abroad because they are South African. Black marathon runners in particular have established an ascendancy in their field – in free competition with Whites – but other Blacks are denying them the opportunity of international recognition. Could H G Wells's famous aphorism apply here – "moral indignation is jealousy with a halo"?

There was the visit to South Africa of a small party of Dublin shop assistants on an anti-apartheid campaign. Suffice to say that most people would doubt whether the unhappinesses of that troubled island offer useful lessons in co-existence and non-violence. I say this in all humility being of Irish extraction myself.

It should be a cause for sadness on the part of thinking people the number of innocent people who are swept into the sanctions net. Did United States Congressmen have any thought for the loss of revenue to the Cape Verde Islands when they summarily called for an immediate end to landing rights for South African Airways. The island of Sal was a regular staging point for SAA on its New York flights, and the cancellation of the service (without, it might be added, the required period of notice) has robbed the Cape Verde islanders, who are certainly not among the world's wealthy people, of valuable revenue. One could suspect that those who have knee-jerk reaction to what they judge to be a moral situation don't always do their homework. Perhaps the USA has offered compensation; I have not come upon a report to this effect.

"Man's inhumanity to man" certainly seems to find some reflection in the application of sanctions against South Africa. It has been reported in our local press that Swedish sanctions have nearly crippled a Lutheran Church project to employ and care for disabled Zulus at a Natal mission station.

For the past decade, according to the Johannesburg *Sunday Times*, communion wafers baked at the KwaZamokuhle Mission just outside Estcourt in the Natal highlands have been exported to Sweden, bringing about R10 000 a year. But the head of the mission said that the wafers had been categorised as a food by the Swedish government and are banned in terms of anti-South African sanctions.

"We used the profits from the bakery", she said, "to help support our health clinic, a protected workshop for disabled people and a boarding establishment for disabled black schoolchildren".

I wonder what the Swedish translation is of "feelgoodie". Perhaps one can take this as another example of foreign policy being dictated by emotional spasm. Don't the people of these countries feel embarrassed?

The visit to Cape Town in September 1986 of Mrs Coretta Scott King, widow of Dr Martin Luther King, raised all sorts of interesting considerations and seemed an exception to the "pre-prejudiced" visitor to whom we have unfortunately

35

become accustomed. Her visit will best be remembered, one fears, for a diplomatic gaffe she made in not keeping an appointment with the South African State President and only letting him know by letter later. She also failed to keep an appointment with the acting Minister of Foreign Affairs. Despite the affront offered, I think that many South Africans have sympathy with this gentle woman who came out to South Africa, one presumes in good faith, to see the situation for herself and was to all intents and purposes hijacked, or call it blackmailed. Dr Alan Boesak, who has ridden many headlines in recent times, and Mrs Winnie Mandela threatened that they would not see her if she saw President Botha. In her letter to President Botha, Mrs King wrote that she was deeply pained about the fact that she had been subjected to extraordinary local and international pressure since she arrived in South Africa. In a subsequent statement, Mrs King said: "I came to South Africa in a Christ-like spirit to gather additional information about the human sufferings here and the need to have dialogue with as many South Africans as possible. After being in South Africa for a week, I now feel I need more time to acquire a better understanding of the complex problems here in order to have a more substantive meeting with President Botha."

The State President's office summed it up in a statement:

The State President intended to inform Mrs King that the prevailing conditions in Crossroads were the result of an orchestrated attempt by the UDF (the United Democratic Front, of which Dr Boesak is patron) to keep people there. Dr Boesak took a lead in this. During his visit in January 1985, Senator Edward Kennedy advised the inhabitants not to move, although he described Crossroads as one of the worst townships he had ever seen. In spite of invitations, Senator Kennedy refused to visit Khayelitsha, and Mrs King and her entourage have not visited Khayelitsha either.

In view of the attempts by Archbishop Desmond Tutu and others to keep Mrs King uninformed and to hold the real state of affairs from her, Mr Botha intended to give her facts about Khayelitsha. These were that as many as 5 136 houses had already been built in the township; 17 912 serviced sites had been provided; there was a secondary school with 14 primary schools, and a further six primary schools would be ready in November.

From January 1985 to the present, as many as 12 500 sites had been developed – an average of 625 a month, the statement said. Three community centres, six clinics and two shopping complexes had been erected.

At this stage, housing is already being provided for approximately 126 500 people, and the Government has already spent R139 million on this development.

(One might insinuate the thought here that those United States Blacks living in the squalid conditions that I have seen for myself on visits over there should ask some of the American radicals and do-gooders to sponsor them on a visit to South Africa to see what our authorities are doing in the way of urban housing. At the same time, they should bear in mind that, on a comparative basis, the problem is much greater in South Africa.)

Zulu leader Dr Buthelezi was critical of Archbishop Desmond Tutu and Dr Boesak whom he accused of pressurising Mrs King into cancelling meetings with President Botha and himself. He doubtless spoke for a majority of South Africans, both Black and White, when he said it was tragic that the memory of Dr Martin Luther King was now being tainted by the action of Black South Africans who were using him as a party-political weapon in seeking advantages in the political feuding dividing South African Blacks.

Another indication of the misinformation to which Mrs King was subjected was evident at the news conference she gave on her return to Washington. She was reported as saying that she had postponed her meeting with President Botha because several Black leaders had felt that it was "too soon after the terrible violence at Soweto and too close to the pending execution of anti-apartheid protesters". This is a favourite and well-perpetuated canard of the anti-apartheid lobby, that you are permitted to commit any crime, even murder, and expect immunity because you are protesting against apartheid. Committing a crime, even if you claim political motivation, does not absolve you from the processes of the law. There is no such thing as the death penalty simpy for political protest.

Mrs King was in Cape Town during "Honour our Seniors" week. It is an annual event organised by the Cape Peninsula Organisation for the Aged, of which I happen to be a Council member, so I was very much in on the event. I wish Mrs King had been there to see what went on and to sense the atmosphere. A very substantial number of those taking part (possibly a majority) were from our Coloured and Black communities – CPOA being an organisation that serves all population groups. Mrs King, I am sure, would have been warmed by the happy atmosphere that was engendered, the natural and spontaneous mixing, and the strong self-help motivation on the part of the respective communities. For anyone looking for the creation of a "normal society" in South Africa, it was there for Mrs King and all to see.

I have purposely dealt with Mrs King's contretemps in some detail because, to those outside South Africa who are reliant on news reports, things are not always what they seem. The simplistic notion of Whites just being nasty to Blacks is way out.

But what of sanctions? Have its advocates thought out the implications not only for South Africans (the Blacks being the first to feel the pinch) and for South Africa's immediate neighbours and the region as a whole, but also for South Africa's trading partners for whom the South African connection provides thousands of jobs?

A question that seems to have early on been lost in all the emotion is "Who foots the bill for losses sustained by those imposing sanctions against South Africa?" Will it be those who were and are most vocal in their demand for sanctions? Seemingly some of the African states would like to have their cake and eat it. Will the well-worn African begging bowl continue to be produced? The British Prime Minister, Mrs Thatcher, according to reports, put it this way: "If you want to cut your throats, don't come to me for a bandage." Even if she was misquoted, the sentiment presumably still stands.

South Africa's immediate Black neighbouring states, as well as Zambia and Zaire, will remain dependent on South Africa and its infrastructure and its technical expertise for years to come, despite large-scale funding by certain foreign governments to make these countries less dependent on South Africa.

Despite anti-South African invective, South Africa is still trading with other parts of Africa, to the tune of an estimated R300 million last year, during which some 800 businessmen from other African countries visited South Africa. Johannesburg has become "the New York" of Africa.

If an epidemic happens outside our borders, whether it be medical or veterinary, South Africa as before can be relied upon to give instant assistance with vaccines. In September 1987, a South African expert acted as an adviser at a conference in Europe on African horse sickness, and Spain subsequently ordered 25 000 doses of vaccine from the Onderstepoort laboratories outside Pretoria.

We treat patients from other African countries in our hospitals – 1 398 in the past year received specialist care, including those from the so-called front-line states.

We provide jobs for many thousands of foreign Blacks.

With 60 per cent of Africa's generating capacity, we supply electricity to neighbouring states, and they earn a substantial revenue from the South African Customs Union.

Certain African airlines make use of the technical and training facilities at Jan Smuts airport outside Johannesburg.

South Africa is to spend R3 million to improve facilities at Maputo harbour in Moçambique so that more use may be made of it for exports.

It is ironic that Zimbabwe, one of the foremost advocates of sanctions, had almost immediately to ask its southern neighbour to help it by supplying 34 000 tons of fuel because of "difficulty" at home – and they had to follow it up with a request for another 8 000 tons. It goes without saying that it would be South African railway trucks that would do the transporting. The General Manager of the South African Transport Services said in a television interview in February 1987 that at any one time there are about 7 500 SATS railway trucks in neighbouring territories.

The United States has had to exempt ten South African minerals from its sanctions list because of the strategic implications.

One day people over there will have to rethink the effectiveness of sanctions. The 1980 grain embargo imposed by the Carter administration against the Soviet Union in protest at the invasion of Afghanistan finds the Russians still there. As an American business expert put it: "They just found other sources of grain. The American farmer suffered the most."

A significant point was made in a speech by Dr Cedric Phatudi, the distinguished Chief Minister of the self-governing territory of Lebowa shortly before his death in October 1987. He said that trade should not be viewed as a favour that a beneficent America or United Kingdom or any other country bestows on other nations, but rather as a thoroughly practical policy that leads to international prosperity and a reduction in tensions.

An odd paradox was thrown up in trade figures for a six-month period in the application of sanctions against South Africa by the United States. Between January and July 1987, the total financial value of US imports from South Africa was reported as having fallen dramatically by 45 per cent to $654 million as against $1 191 million for the same period last year.

However, SA Customs and Excise figures reveal that our total exports for the first seven months of 1987 showed a trade surplus of R8 300 million against R7 730 million for the same period of 1986. There is food for thought here both for those who rushed hell-bent into imposing sanctions and those who did not believe in the first place that they would have the contemplated effect.

Recent reports indicate that the United States is to lift sanctions imposed on Poland in 1981, partly because Lech Walesa and Archbishop Glemp have claimed that the measures have not affected the regime but meant hardship for the people.

This has a familiar ring about it, because as I said earlier in this chapter, the first to feel the pinch in South Africa have been the Blacks whom sanctions have been aimed to help. As far as the South African government is concerned, it is being slowed in its reform commitment – another contradictory factor in the application of sanctions.

Dr Mangosuthu Buthelezi, Chief Minister of KwaZulu, puts it in a nutshell: "Black workers who were politically duped into supporting a tactic they barely understood are now facing the brunt of yet another failed African National Congress strategy . . . the very people who travelled the world campaigning for disinvestment and sanctions still have their jobs while the victims of disinvestment and sanctions are losing theirs in droves." Dr Buthelezi made his standpoint clear: "I oppose disinvestment and sanctions as vehemently as I oppose the South African Government."

In another statement, he said: "There is a growing perception amongst Black South Africans that we must negotiate and, short of bringing about change through a bloody and violent revolution, we have to negotiate with the South African Government."

The withdrawal of American firms from South Africa has left an unhappy sequel. A market research organisation specialising in Black social and political research has found that Blacks are starting to feel "deserted" by international companies whose withdrawals were leaving unemployment in their wake. The report says that Blacks now see international companies as "less than perfect in employment terms and definitely not better than their South African equivalents – despite the Sullivan code. Many Black workers now

41

suspect disinvestment moves were motivated by economic rather than altruistic reasons".

Apart from its effect on various social programmes designed to improve conditions among the Black communities, this corporate retreat is likely to persuade Blacks that big business is a faint-hearted ally when it comes to social and political reform.

In contrast, it was an agreeable surprise to read of the recent establishment in Washington DC of an organisation of Black businessmen, one of whose aims is helping South African businessmen of colour. The Resolve Through Commerce Foundation is to concentrate its attentions on Third World countries, and one of its first projects is to open an office in Johannesburg to establish contacts . . . proof that more people are "getting the message" that one of the most powerful weapons against apartheid is economics.

Is it not time that the more experienced nations who up to now have "played along" in the African charade took another look at the situation? To introduce a sympathetic note, it is not inconceivable that Africa's problems are so huge and complex and seemingly insoluble that African leaders have been conditioned not to recognise them. In round figures, it is 25 years since the end of the colonial era in Africa, and in an article in 1985 in his London-based magazine *Africa Now*, Peter Enahoro (himself a Black) was not impressed with what had been achieved. "Blaming colonialism and its aftermath of covert imperialism is not only popular among us Africans," he wrote, "it is *de rigueur* in successful academic and political circles."

Mr Enahoro harked back to the immediate post-colonial years of the 1960's when African countries became adept at arousing the conscience of their erstwhile colonial masters: "To put it bluntly, we blackmailed the hell out of the liberalism sweeping Western Europe. We seized upon the Cold War rivalries (for once playing clever) and teased the great powers by switching flirtations . . ."

The time is surely long past for the blackmailing to stop, and for the Western nations to point out to those African countries that are high on rhetoric that someone has to pay the bill. Bluster and threats, not least from the prima donnas of the new Commonwealth, should by this time have had their day, and nowhere more than in Africa should the maxim apply "Put your money where your mouth is."

By their indulgence, Western nations are actually doing Africa a disservice by cloaking reality. The West needs to inject a strong dose of practicality and realism and to point out to various African countries that their own self-interest should dictate a change in attitude to South Africa. I would even go so far as to hazard the guess that the states of southern Africa are ripe for negotiation in the interests of the region as a whole. If the recent successful exchange of prisoners involving France, the Netherlands, Angola, the UNITA movement, Ciskei and South Africa (which took place on Moçambique soil) is anything to go by, a bit more perseverance between parties of goodwill could yield dramatic results. It could be the sort of "revolution" that southern Africa really needs.

Moçambique is an interesting case in point. Before independence, it was a favourite holiday venue for South Africans and Rhodesians who poured millions of escudos into the economy. Now it is torn by civil strife, the economy is in ruins, and the once attractive city of Lourenço Marques (now Maputo) is a mess. Nor can it be said that the population of Moçambique is better off, or happier, than when it was a Portuguese province. For what? An ideal? Given the right circumstances, we South Africans would be back again in our thousands because it is the nearest sea to the enormous conurbation of Johannesburg and only a few hours drive away. Thousands of us remember eating prawns and drinking that lovely Portuguese green wine at the many cafes and restaurants that used to flourish and that gave young South Africans their first introduction to a continental style of life. Angola had the same tourist potential. I remember Luanda as a most delightful and picturesque city magnificently sited on its bay. And now? Angola could also have reaped a rich harvest from South African tourist revenue that now flows to Mauritius and elsewhere.

There is much talk abroad about South Africa's "destabilising" of its neighbours. This, and other types of criticism, is usually indulged in, it would seem, by people who understand as little about the complexities of southern Africa as they do about the reasons for the long drawn out and bloody war between Iran and Iraq. To put it succinctly, South Africa is protecting itself from those across its borders who wish it harm.

However, to be brutally frank, a lot of this so-called destabilisation – apart from natural disasters – can be blamed on these African states' inability to conduct their own affairs properly, and on a pan-African ideal that has little chance of realisation. South Africa is a convenient scapegoat. At the 1987 annual summit conference of the Organisation of African Unity (OAU) days were reportedly spent on a ritualistic condemnation of South Africa and a call for sanctions while large parts of the continent are dying and disintegrating because of drought, mismanagement, corruption and political instability. It was also reported that fewer than 20 heads of state attended the conference.

Again, looking at the situation sympathetically, one is aware that the situation throughout Africa is aggravated by historical factors, tribal rivalries and antipathies and other factors, and the situation is not helped – as I implied – by the indulgences of Western nations. It suits some people (legislators included) to draw moral and political and even emotional sustenance from their uncritical attitudes to palpable absurdities. In their case, sympathy is far from being matched by common sense. The long-surviving "colonial guilt complex" needs to be looked at again and the question to be asked "Where would many African states be today in the matter of infrastructure, health services, and many other benefits had it not been for colonial 'exploitation'?" Incidentally, it has been said of Africa that there is only one thing worse than being exploited by a multinational, and that is *not* being exploited by a multi-national! Certainly the "exploited Blacks" of South Africa are much better off than the vast majority of their Black brothers in

44

other parts of Africa, which is why we have such an influx of "illegals" from other southern African countries.

Another question that needs to be asked is why the economies of so many African countries continue to decline despite large-scale foreign aid. Africa is strewn with remains of development projects that failed, not least in the vital sphere of agriculture, and paranoia about South Africa's alleged wickednesses is not going to improve the situation. Throughout Africa there has been an over-accenting of politics as against economics, and the slogan "Seek ye first the political kingdom" will remain associated with the name of Kwame Nkrumah, one of the first failed African leaders.

People abroad should be under no illusion. Foreign aid, vital and humanitarian as it may be, does carry the risk of being counter-productive in respect of building up a reliance on imported foodstuffs and machinery to the prejudice of indigenous ingenuity, enterprise and effort. Again one excludes natural disasters like drought or floods.

Western nations which genuinely want to see development and economic progress in southern Africa, with peace and stability as a hoped-for corollary, would be better advised to recognise South Africa's established rôle as the leading nation in the region, and one moreover that has a vested interest in progress in the region. South Africa has repeatedly expressed its wish to cooperate fully in this respect – and, be it noted, it has no territorial ambitions.

Instead of pouring vast amounts of money piecemeal into what appears to be a bottomless pit, the West should take a co-ordinated approach to try to ensure that funds allotted are used to the best advantage and not just frittered away – and that "humanitarian aid" does not find its way into the pockets of arms dealers. By involving South Africa's African know-how, as well as its comprehensive infrastructure and sophisticated economy, there might be some prospect at long last of achieving social and economic lift-off for the region as a whole.

But – and this is an important but – the Western nations should make it clear that the ideological and woolly dream of a happy workers' paradise under a Marxist, socialist regime, is out – it has repeatedly been found wanting. The West should hold up as an example the experience of the Republic of China (Taiwan) which, within only a few decades, has transformed its population from Third World to First World status – and, in the process, has become one of the world's most dynamic economies. Their success can be attributed to what might be termed "people's capitalism".

It is significant that all this was achieved under a continuous state of martial law which, after 38 years, was lifted in 1987. In the same year, the Prime Minister of South Korea (which also has an interesting economy) threatened action against Communist supporters who cause labour unrest in a bid to bring about violent revolution. A motto for Africa could well be "No progress without stability."

Another case, nearer home, is Malawi which has written its own success story despite its lack of Westminster-style "democracy".

At this point I want to mention two books that offer valuable insights into the South African situation. One is *Priorities for Coexistence* by Anton Rupert, and the other is *Anton Rupert: Advocate of Hope* by W P Esterhuyse, both published by Tafelberg. As South Africans will know, Dr Rupert is an Afrikaans industrial magnate with world wide contacts and he has for years been expressing – positively and not negatively – viewpoints opposed to current government policies. He made history in 1963 by breaking through the wage barrier and establishing a basic minimum wage for all employees of his vast industrial empire. This was an early reflection of his pre-occupation with enlightened employment practices which is part of his broad and generous social philosophy. This has embraced, among many other manifestations, the Lesotho medical shuttle scheme whereby South African medical specialists and nursing personnel fly in periodically to this mountain kingdom to conduct an intensive week-end of consultations and operations. The medical contingent offer their services free, and the other costs are met by Dr Rupert.

If one were to attempt to classify him in the glib way in which we hang labels round people's necks, he inevitably would be categorised as a liberal – but not in the narrow and inaccurate definition often applied in South Africa. While he does not see apartheid as the sole guarantee of White survival, he does not take the common simplistic interpretation of one-man-one-vote as providing the key to stability. He poses the question "Where in the world has a country undergone a successful industrial revolution under a system of equal voting rights? It did not happen in Germany or Japan, nor in England or America." This is not expressing opposition to universal suffrage, but to oppose the notion that one-man-one-vote is the key to development and that it will necessarily lead to progress and greater participation in prosperity. Development, he believes, is stimulated not by the right to political self-determination but by the freedom to participate in the economy.

And here we come to Dr Rupert's key philosophy – the philosophy of partnership.

Reading *Anton Rupert: Advocate of Hope* and *Priorities for Coexistence* is almost to be persuaded that politics is too important to be left to politicians.

Going back to the sanctions issue, it is interesting to find that more than one side is now developing to the question of boycotts.

According to a December 1986 report from Washington DC, large American corporations being boycotted for continuing to trade in South Africa are retaliating with boycotts of their own. Some of the companies are withholding grants, scholarships and bonuses from American universities and colleges that have chosen, or threaten, to divest their shares in the companies. One corporation has cut grants to six institutions and threatened similar action against others. A spokesman said "If our corporation isn't good enough for you, you aren't good enough for our corporation." A business executive is reported as saying that if the schools want

47

to be moral about South Africa, they should refuse donations from the companies that operate there.

On this whole subject of sanctions against South Africa, a cautionary thought was expressed in July 1986 by the Chairman of the giant Anglo American Corporation of South Africa, Gavin Relly. It sums up the situation:

The Western world must not allow itself to be pressured into adopting punitive measures which would undermine both the transitional phase and the success of South Africa's post-apartheid society.

The West, as much as South Africa, needs to take decisions that are soundly informed by a strategic vision of their long-term consequences. Any action taken now, primarily in an emotional response to the gravity of the situation here, is bound to be at the expense of freedom and justice in South Africa, for if our nascent and fragile democratic institutions are denied a strong economic underpinning, they will certainly give way to tyranny.

Even Mrs Helen Suzman, that doughty campaigner against apartheid in the South African Parliament, has said that those in the West who support punitive sanctions overlook two key points: the form of rule that might follow in the aftermath of a downfall of the current government, and that a growing number of Whites support the dismantling of apartheid. She said "There are no guarantees that it (the present South African government) would be replaced by a non-racial democracy respecting the rule of law."

It is increasingly being recognised, happily in some overseas circles as well, that the final nails in the apartheid coffin will be supplied by strong economic growth that will absorb all elements of society. Economic strength on the part of the Blacks will promote political leverage. That being the case, boycotts and sanctions can only prove counter-productive and destroy the good work that has been done, not least by those overseas firms in South Africa that have had a strong social commitment along with their earning of substantial profits.

It is an unfortunate aspect of the current situation that,

while we in South Africa appreciate the veto exercised in the United Nations Security Council by the United States and others over too-radical measures aimed at this country, the attitude and activities of, say, the United States Congress in its sanctions policy, with its implied support of the revolutionary forces seeking the overthrow of the South African government, can be argued as actually impeding the process of reform by undermining the position of moderate Black leaders. It could also be argued that the African National Congress is only succeeding in slowing up Black "liberation". It will be the Blacks who suffer the hangover from the emotional binge that many parts of the world have been enjoying.

I am ending this chapter with the words of an overseas observer who visited South Africa in recent months. He is a doctor in Toronto who was one of 64 Canadians on a fact-finding tour of this country. In a perceptive article in the *Toronto Star* headed "The Good Side of White South Africa", he concluded:

> . . . I left South Africa with one certainty. Economic sanctions, disinvestment and the boycotting of goods merely set the stage for more black unemployment and unrest. It's the wrong medication for the wrong country at the wrong time. And if a bloodbath does occur, ill-informed churchmen, do-gooders, hypocrites who judge the Third World by a Western moral code, naïve politicians and irresponsible media will all have helped to pull the trigger.

THE MEDIA

News is anything that makes you say gee whiz.

A question asked at a symposium was "What is the first priority of a newpaper?" One answer, which apparently surprised many of those present (who doubtless expected something more lofty), was "To make a profit".

I want to start by suggesting that all news emanations, whether by way of newspaper, television or radio, be required to make a declaration on the lines of a government health warning on smoking: "This news is liable to be dangerous to your understanding."

This is not an "attack" on the media (although that is a word much beloved of them) but rather an attempt to recognise that there is a prime need for the public at large to recognise how the media work; to appreciate that in a sense they are all selling a product and to be able to identify a shoddy product when they encounter one. I have advocated for a long time that all secondary schools should have a course on "understanding the media" to give young people going out in the world a better chance of appreciating the parameters within which the media operate.

If I can risk being facetious, one can imagine a schoolteacher explaining to the class: "No, that headline 'Tragedy at Loftus' did not mean that the big rugby stand in Pretoria had collapsed with loss of life; merely that Northern Transvaal had been beaten on their home ground. 'City Demolished' did not mean that Cape Town had been hit by an earthquake; merely that the local soccer team had lost their match by a big margin."

I am not cavilling at the normal business of news and information dissemination, nor at the provision of editorial comment and other comment by authoritative and responsible columnists. This is a newspaper's or magazine's pre-

50

rogative, and most do an admirable job, and who would be without them? But where the press blurs the boundaries between news and comment; when it enters the field of speculative thumb-sucking and omniscience (headline: "Whites have Acute Crisis of Confidence in their Future"); of high moral tone and muck-raking in the guise of social concern; of political king-making, then I get a little twitchy about the Fourth Estate. Incidentally, there is an unusual word *haruspication* which means divination from the entrails of animals. I suspect that, over the years, a fair amount of what I have read in newspapers could be attributable to that source, which is possibly also the origin of the "gut feeling" that some journalists lay claim to.

As I have implied, I am not impugning the journalistic profession as a whole (or the media at large), but if the public is buying its product, then the public needs to be aware of that important Latin tag *caveat emptor* – let the buyer beware.

In the last chapter, I mentioned Crossroads, the big squatter camp outside Cape Town. The world has heard a lot about this place. Some years ago, in the earlier days of Crossroads before the awful internecine violence of 1986 when Blacks were murdering Blacks, I had a telexed request asking me to give whatever assistance I could to two French television men who wanted to do a preliminary survey for a possible series of television features on South Africa. They could spend only two days in Cape Town and wanted to see as much as possible in the time.

I met them at the airport, took them smartly up Table Mountain (which I felt they should not miss) and then I concentrated on what I felt they would want to see, and that is the Black and Coloured areas. I parked the car on the sandy verge of the road running past Crossroads and we walked into this already large Black squatter camp that was growing every day and had already made world news. It was a bleak expanse of sand dunes, not far from the airport, with a low-lying sprawl of shacks and shanties made of old sheet iron, bits of sacking, cardboard tacked onto odd bits of timber . . . anything and everything. There were widely separated taps, bucket sanitation only, no roads as such . . . just a very primitive squatter camp that had suddenly mushroomed. But life was going on. Some of the shacks had quite good furniture, double beds and suchlike; there were a few cars parked among the scrubby trees, and small businesses had been established in an alfresco way, as you will see all over Africa. There was a rudimentary butcher shop selling cheap cuts of meat.

Everywhere we went we encountered a friendly greeting "Hello, come inside." They didn't know who we were; they weren't wanting to make statements to the foreign media or anything like that. There was just the normal human warmth and friendliness that is such a wonderful trait of our Black people.

Well, we spent half an hour in Crossroads looking at every aspect. As we got back into the car, the French television director (the other one was the writer-to-be of this series on South Africa) said to me: "You know, I could make a television film on Crossroads that would make people cry. But it wouldn't be true."

The moral is here for anyone to digest.

People visiting South Africa, some of them clearly stamped as professional propagandists, have said that they are "offended" by places like Crossroads. On my visits to the United States, I have seen some quite ghastly slums, some of them in the nation's capital itself, but I have never said "I am offended by them." There seemed to be slim grounds for me, as an outsider, to be "offended" by something in another country. Is this not the prerogative of Americans? I include their racial situation as well, and the inequities that go with it. I talked to enough Blacks in the United States to be under no illusions, but at the same time I would have imagined that there would be enough people of concern and conscience in the United States not to need prodding by an outsider to rectify the ills of their society. Or am I not a busybody at heart?

Let me quote another personal experience of the parameters within which the news media work.

In the 1960's I was in Europe recording programmes for the SABC and I had the chance of watching South Africa's Davis Cup team play the Netherlands at Scheveningen. The tennis that day was not particularly good or exciting, but that evening, having drinks with friends in Amsterdam, the television happened to be on and there on the screen was an edited version of the day's play in this Cup tie . It was an exciting fifteen or twenty minutes, with aces, brilliant passing shots, staggering net play – all one could wish for in a day's play. But it was very different from my recollection . . . in a manner of speaking it wasn't true. Needless to say, the exciting bits had been extracted for the edited version which, in the final analysis, was a distortion of the actual event. Irresponsible on the part of the television people, or not? What was the alternative – pick out the dull bits and string them together? That is one of the limitations within which the media work. But even making allowance for that, there is undeniable degree of chicanery that goes on in the media, some of which is directed against South Africa.

At a dinner in Cape Town in 1963 to celebrate the 25th anniversary of the South African Press Association, the then Prime Minister, Dr. H.F. Verwoerd, as guest of honour, said in his speech that if western civilisation were to disappear, he had no doubt that a finger would be pointed at the press and news agencies by some future historians in assessing the blame. He spoke, incidentally, as a former newspaper editor himself. He went on to say: "One must think of the way in which ideologies opposing the western world and our way of thought are trying to undermine us, not by means of armed power but by undermining the minds of the people and their confidence in themselves." Of course he could have added radio and television to this indictment. But it is all too easy to get uptight about the media. Can anyone visualise not having newspapers or radio or television or magazines? To take one example; although investigative journalism may be uncomfortable to certain people, when handled with responsibility and honesty it plays an important rôle in a well ordered society, with the proviso – anathema, one imagines, to some journalists' dogged professionalism – that a secret made available to all is available to enemies as well as friends.

But inevitably the media enlarge the area of conflict. Flying back from the United States on one occasion, I picked up a copy of a Johannesburg newspaper which was among a batch of South African papers that the aircraft had brought across for the benefit of us southbound passengers. In it I read an item headlined "Man stoned to death in Boston race war". Well, I had been following this story in the American press and on television, and by no stretch of any reasonable imagination could the label "race war" be attached to it. It was no doubt journalistically pleasing as a headline, but not a reflection of the situation. So, one might ask, "Who are they kidding?".

On another occasion, I came down by cargo ship from Mombasa to Durban. It was a leisurely ten-day voyage during which I didn't see a single newspaper or listen to the radio. So, imagine my degree of surprise, not to say alarm, to see a bold headline flashed across the front page of the first newspaper I bought on landing "War Possible". I thought to myself "What's been happening while I've been at sea?" But it was a false alarm. The headline concerned an analysis of the situation in Europe by the then Prime Minister of Great Britain in which he ended with words to the effect that as in all circumstances war is always possible. But this was sufficient to spark a dramatic headline, and it probably sold more newspapers that day.

It is commonly said that news is anything that makes you say "Gee whiz". Also that good news is no news. And it is worth remembering what has been said before: "The law of life is that there is always *less* going on than meets the eye."

Cast your memory back to the period of widespread student unrest in the United States. The fountainhead of a lot of the disturbance was the Berkeley campus of the University of California, just across the bay from San Francisco, which constantly figured in dramatic reports reaching the world press. I was over there some years later when the rash of student unrest had spread eastwards across the Atlantic and I recorded the comments of a number of members of faculty as well as students. One of them was Professor Martin Trow, Professor of Sociology in the Graduate School of Public Policy, and this is what he told me.

I think that the degree of disturbance was exaggerated largely by the press, probably because they report what is interesting and exciting and pay little attention to the kind of ongoing routine parts of life that aren't exciting. But even during the worst of the disturbances on campus, most of the Universities were in full operation – 90 to 95 per cent of the students were going to their classes, faculty members were meeting their classes and carrying on with their research and scholarship. One never would have dreamt that from the television programmes or the newspapers. You would have gotten the idea that the Universities were on the brink of closure and the country was on the brink of revolution. That's just nonsense.

So, on the premise that good news is no news, what the world hears of South Africa is accurate within certain limits, but is often grossly lacking in perspective. There is no doubt that the media at large have become factories of the emotions, and perhaps to those who don't think very deeply, they have become emotional dictators with their creation of "instant" villains and "instant" heroes. But these "instant" images don't necessarily bring instant comprehension. What one gets instead tends to be instant myth. As far as television is concerned, there is no doubt that its pictures are stronger in arousing emotions than in cultivating rationality.

Dr Bryan Wilson, Reader in Sociology in the University of Oxford and a Fellow of All Souls, makes this comment in his book *The Youth Culture and the Universities*.

There can be no doubt that the general public has an avid appetite for the criminal, the violent, the salacious, and the sensational. But in just what measure it may indulge these appetites depends to a very considerable extent on the values of our mass media, for it is the mass media which themselves establish the degree of "permissiveness". There has been a competitive catering to these appetites and a deliberate stimulation of a public interest by creating "sensations". The appetite is no doubt there in the public, but it is the media which have stimulated it as they have vied with each other in the presentation of material to satisfy it. Employing the specious rationalisation that the "public has a right to know", they have extended the range of subjects which can be freely discussed, so that the issues that thirty years ago were more or less unmentionable are, today, almost casually discussed in the press. They have built up around the sensational a cult of spurious sentiment by interviewing the relatives of victims and seeking statements from anyone connected with the central characters of a crime. Even the BBC has resorted to this trading on sentiment and sensation – no doubt aware of its need to compete in these directions in order to hold an audience. Frequently, this approach is accompanied by expressions of moral concern; sometimes, indeed, "exposures" are justified by the expression of moral indignation on the part of the reporters. For some newspapers, and some television programmes, this is an almost stock pattern for the presentation of material which otherwise might be "too hot to handle".

On a less serious note, one can cite the criticism that grew up around Jackie Kennedy and even our own Professor Christian Barnard. "Oh, they're such publicity seekers . . ." This is nonsense. I know Chris Barnard and had a lot to do with him in the early days of heart transplantation, and far from his being a publicity seeker, the media sought him out to the point of making his life uncomfortable. I doubt whether he is unhappy with the personal publicity that he has generated, but to say that he sought it is a travesty of the facts. I remember the time of the first human heart transplant when Groote Schuur Hospital and the adjacent Medical School became a bear garden with media reporters almost breaking down doors to get their stories. I have no doubt that the same thing applies to Jackie Kennedy

Onassis. Take the case of Princess Anne. Why has she the reputation for disliking the press? Because some elements overstep reasonable norms in invading her privacy.

There was a classic case of the specious invocation of "the public's right to know" during the Vietnam war when a film crew of the United States CBS network (which does not have a noteworthy record of probity in its activities in South Africa, nor, I understand, in its own country) was on hand to film the actual moment when military personnel arrived at the home of a United States marine to report to his family that he had been killed. This film sequence actually went out on the air, though the programme's anchorman had the grace to apologise, saying that the film should not have been shown as it was "inappropriate". But in the eyes of some television practitioners, that would have ranked as "good television".

I feel sorry for young people these days who must sense the tremendous clash between the old precepts of thought and moral principle that they may still encounter at home and at school and at church, with the new morality taught by some of the media. It is curious that, in some reporting, criminals and mobsters become almost romantic figures – witness the case of train robber Ronald Biggs who was pursued with money offers to "tell all"; when his Brazilian girl friend became pregnant in a transparent move for him to claim asylum, he was invested with an even more romantic aura. There is no doubt that the media are adept at making celebrities out of nonentities, provided they have something sensational or destructive to put across; all too often this masquerades as serious social comment. Very often governments and other statutory bodies are put at a disadvantage in the face of dramatic, emotional (even irresponsible) allegations or attacks by the public; these make good headlines, but official bodies cannot react with the same degree of emotion, and so appear to lose the argument by default.

What one might term "manufactured news" is a useful stock-in-trade for elements of the media . . . what one

American newspaper editor himself described as "junk dressed up to look as meaningful as the real news". Many people will remember the death of United Nations Secretary-General Dag Hammarskjöld in an air crash while on his way to attempt to mediate in the dispute between the Congo and its secessionist province of Katanga. Many newspapers throughout the world carried reports of his meeting at Ndola with Moise Tshombe. There were colourful details about the airport, the aircraft landing, the departure in separate cars for a secret rendezvous, and so on. Meanwhile, Dag Hammarskjöld lay dead in his crashed aircraft. How does one explain that sort of thing? Easy. These reporters/correspondents go out on expensive assignments and are under pressure to "get the goods" and where possible to scoop the opposition. But . . . *caveat emptor!*

Leaving aside the many anti-South African stories that are cooked up by the overseas media in the fairly reasonable knowledge that they will stick ("give a dog a bad name" and all that sort of thing), there is the interesting case of the writer on *The Washington Post* who was forced to return a Pulitzer Prize when she had to admit that she had invented the title character of a portrait she had written of an 8-year old heroin addict. *The Washington Post* has had a lot to say about South Africa.

Manufactured news also occurs in the useful stratagem of one comment generating another comment . . . "We asked so-and-so-for comment . . ." and so on. I am always rather morbidly fascinated by the free publicity that is given to terrorist and other subversive organisations in media reports. . . "Such-and-such an organisation claimed responsibility" for an outrage, so presumably in their eyes this publicity is valuable. The *Mini-manual of the Urban Guerilla* written by the Brazilian revolutionary Carlos Marighella makes it clear how the media (unwitting as it may be to them) can be harnessed into promoting the terrorist cause. Thus can comfort be offered to a country's enemies.

These days, in the face of intense competition for circulation, listenership or viewership, some elements of the media are not too scrupulous, as I suggested earlier, in the matter of accuracy, being confident that an anti-South African story has a good chance of being credited abroad. So you come on media reports of "bombing raids against the capitals of three of its neighbours . . ." These referred to the pinpoint take-out of African National Congress bases in adjoining territories from which terror raids were being launched with Communist weapons against "soft" targets in South Africa.

Rational thinking goes adrift in the matter of terrorism. Those same people who applauded the United States bombing of Libya deplore pre-emptive action by South Africa to protect its population from terrorist incursions across its borders. Much talk and some action is being deployed in trying to eradicate terrorism world-wide, but moral and material support is being offered by Western countries to the ANC for its indiscriminate attacks here in South Africa. Are we all becoming so inured to news reports of violent incidents that they don't mean as much these days? It is when a name you know appears in a report that the news really hits home.

Some time ago, I had a small job done on my house by a builder who ran his own small contracting business. I gave him my cheque, and two days later I read in the newspaper that he was dead. He had given a lift in his vehicle to some of his Black workmen, and when he stopped to put them down in their township, he was set upon by a Black mob, doused with petrol and set alight. He had been doing his Black workmen a favour, but he was White . . .

The unrealism of some Western attitudes finds reflection in a review in the London *Observer* newspaper of a new book *Time for Peace* by Peter Calvocoressi. The reviewer was Richard Harries, Dean of King's College, London, and Bishop-elect of Oxford. The review is headed "Defining the Just War" and the book considers various so-called terrorist organisations. One sentence in the review stands out: "Che Guevara distinguished between sabotage and terrorism and so does the ANC." This, of course, is sheer uninformed nonsense; the worthy cleric should have been around when

dead and maimed bodies were flying through the air following ANC bomb blasts. Some would argue that it is just too
bad if civilians get caught in the cross fire, but the targets
selected are all too often "soft", such as shopping centres,
where the victims cannot be other than civilians, including
children.

At one stage during the unrest through which South
Africa has been passing, restrictions were imposed on television crews filming scenes of violence, on the established
premise that this was liable to foment the spread of violence. Although such restrictions are not unknown in other
parts of the world, there was the expectable outcry from the
media about restricting the public's right to know. However,
the desired result was achieved . . . South Africa became less
of a "hot property" for the networks.

Coverage of the situation in South Africa had become an
important element in the ratings war for gathering audi-
ences, almost as in showbiz – as someone put it rather aptly
– South Africa's people turned into actors for street opera.
Once again television proved its ability to blur the distinction between shadow and substance, because during this
time probably 95 per cent of South Africa's people were
going about their normal life quite unaffected by what was
occurring in limited areas. What I am saying is not an
attempt to underplay the seriousness of some of the causes
behind the unrest; there are big issues that need to be
addressed – and they are being addressed. But highly selective reporting can vitiate a community's ability to come to
grips with its problems. I remember the exodus from South
Africa during earlier periods of unrest. People sold up at
short notice and got out "while the going was good", making very considerable financial sacrifices in the process.
Numbers of these returned in due course, wiser and much
poorer, admitting that they had been panicked by sensational (and sometimes hysterical) reporting. For example,
the recent headline I quoted earlier in this chapter "Whites
Have Acute Crisis of Confidence in their Future". Nobody
asked my opinion!

The sensational style of reporting that has appeared in the overseas media had a not unexpected effect on South Africa's tourist trade. I had direct evidence of this from a friend who is a travel agent in New York whose field is round-the-world cruises. She has told me of the difficulty she has had in selling cruises that included South African ports "because it's too dangerous there." Those passengers who have visited Cape Town and Durban on these cruises have been delighted, she told me. Happily, tourism from abroad has been picking up steadily since then, proving perhaps that people are "taken for a ride" by the media only up to a certain point.

In fairness, one has to accept that, in the course of a high-pressured dissemination of news, it is difficult to preserve an accurate context or perspective. So, a headline "73 Black Schools forced to Close" may be factually accurate, but what is not revealed is that something over 7 000 Black schools were functioning normally. As one Chalmers Roberts said, writing in *Newsweek*: "The trouble with daily journalism is that you get so involved with 'Who hit John?' that you never really know why John had his chin out in the first place."

It has been said that there is nothing new under the sun, and, in all objectivity, what has been happening in South Africa is really rather "old hat" in world terms. South Africa's declaration of a state of emergency made big head-lines, but few people reading those headlines would know that Zimbabwe, one of South Africa's most outspoken crit-ics, has had a state of emergency for 20 odd years – and keeps renewing it. To take another example, in July 1986 it was reported that 596 people in India had been jailed that year under legislation permitting imprisonment without trial or charge. In the same month, the Indian government extended the two-year-old ban on the entry of foreigners into troubled Punjab state. Could it be that their thinking paralleled that of the South African government – to keep out those who wish to stir up more trouble? Singapore intro-duced press curbs in 1987 on the grounds of interference in domestic politics.

61

Memories are short because it seems to be forgotten that when the United States invasion of Grenada took place, the media were excluded from the scene. It was reported that there was overwhelming public support for President Reagan on the issue. During the Falklands war, the British government imposed restrictions, though not an outright ban, on the British media. However, that did not stop strategic information filtering through to the enemy.

There is evidence that the public at large is not as keen as might be thought on a constant sniping at and undermining of authority, or on "leaks" that might constitute a "scoop" in journalistic terms but which could be seen to endanger security.

One of the perennial bones of contention is the objectivity or otherwise of news reporting and the degree to which bias comes into the picture. In his book *A Survey of Television* (Heinemann, London 1967), Stuart Hood, who in the early 1960's was Programme Controller of BBC Television, wrote:

What it will do is to strive to be as fair as the political and social climate allows it to be. It will aim at presenting to its viewers the widest possible spectrum of views so that they may inform themselves and, as informed citizens and voters, decide how they wish to live. It will aim at presenting them with an objective news service – or what a given society accepts as such. For there is no such thing as objective news; there are only a number of verifiable facts – facts which can be corroborated. From these, any news service culls a selection according to certain criteria of interest to the public or importance in the life of the citizens. The choice of these facts is, however, highly subjective, being coloured by the political, religious and social assumptions of the society in which the news editors have been brought up. Editorial judgements will vary within that society from group to group and from class to class. There are, however, certain broad assumptions which guide the editorial process – beliefs in certain rights and freedoms, in certain moral values, and in certain conventions. Objective news is objective within these limits.

Anyone can prove this for him- or herself. Have someone provide a news item of, say, a thousand words embracing a good number of facts. Distribute this among half a dozen or so individuals and ask them to condense the thousand words into a "story" for publication of 150 words. The divergent results would be illuminating, with each individual selecting what he or she considers most relevant or important.

Another interesting angle on the objectivity of news was provided by the "progressive" Director-General of the BBC, Sir Hugh Greene, in an address to the International Catholic Association for Radio and Television in Rome in 1965. It was extensively reported at the time and read, inter alia:

> Nor do I believe we should be impartial about certain things like racialism or extreme forms of political belief. Being too good "democrats" in these matters could open the way to the destruction of our democracy itself. I believe a healthy democracy does not evade discussions about what it can never allow if it is to survive. The actions and aspirations of those who proclaim some political and social ideas are so clearly damaging to society, to peace and good order, even in their immediate effects, that to put at their disposal the enormous power of broadcasting would be to conspire with them against society.

If you read this carefully, you will appreciate that this is a very significant statement, viewed against the BBC's long-acquired reputation for impartiality, because it points to impartiality subject to exceptions. Translated into the current SouthAfrican context, the South African Broadcasting Corporation is presumably justified in not putting broadcasting at the disposal of those whose "political and social ideas are clearly damaging to society, to peace and good order". Members of the public can well ask "Who is to be the arbiter on what is damaging etc?" Who would be the arbiter as far as the BBC is concerned? Presumably the Corporation itself, as having the immediate responsibility. This all makes for fascinating argument.

In doing a roundup of opinion in Britain some years ago, one of the questions I put to a number of people was "How well informed is the British public?" This is the answer given to me by Professor H. Trevor Roper, Regius Professor of History in the University of Oxford, now Lord Dacre.

Very well informed, if by information you mean presentation of facts. But there is a difference between information and reflection, between presentation of facts and interpretation of facts. I'm not so sure that the British public – or any other public now – is very good at interpreting the facts. Partly because the facts are so readily interpreted for them before they can even reach them. We have less and less objective presentation of fact and more and more predigested presentation of opinion. And every man thinks that he is well informed when in fact he has merely received somebody else's pattern. This is what gives the media their great power. In the old days, a man had perhaps fewer facts at his disposal but rather a better capacity to suspend judgement on them.

In his book *The Edwardians*, J B Priestley put it this way in writing of the old days: " . . . we were not being continuously machine-gunned by the news. The experts on everything had not begun their regular barrage of dubious information and guesswork". Or, to put it in the words of Bernard Ingham, Mrs Thatcher's press secretary: "The facts seem to matter less these days than what so-called experts think of them."

In effect, value judgements are being made for us by assorted individuals whom – if we knew them – we might or might not trust.

One of the dangers implicit in reporting, when it comes to individuals and particularly politicians, is that they are all too easily passed through a filter of the media's perceptions. Let me give an example. I have had acquaintance for a good number of years with a prominent member of the former official opposition party in parliament. I admire him as a man of probity and undeniably "a good South African". However, when reported in the press he often comes over as a much less admirable character – even an unpatriotic figure, presented, as I have implied, within the framework of the newspaper's own opposition to the government. On the occasions of his television appearances, I sometimes telephone his afterwards to say "Good show, you made a good impression." In fact, on the last occasion, I made the point that, to me, he had placed himself firmly in the middle ground of South Africanism and not, as the opposition press tended to place him, on the questionable fringe.

One remembers the famous aphorism of *Manchester Guardian* editor C P Scott "Comment is free, facts are sacred" which he regarded as the keystone of newspaper practice. Reacting to that, Nicholas Tomalin, writing in the London *Sunday Times* magazine, had this to say:

This idea is adequate only at the data processing level of journalism. For anyone more talented than a news agency man, the idea of a "fact" is so simplistic it is a lie. Facts are not sacred; the moment any reporter begins to write his story, he has selected some and not others and has distorted the situation. The moment he composes the "facts" into narrative form he has commented on the situation. The idea of "facts" to be shoved at readers like little lumps is best forgotten very swiftly.

To say a journalist's job is to record facts is like saying an architect's job is to lay bricks – true, but missing the point. A journalist's real function, at any rate, his required talent is the creation of interest.

The trouble is that journalism in Britain is crucially divided. Half, or three quarters, or perhaps even seven eights of it, is a service industry, shovelling out perishable facts and names just as the United Dairies deliver milk. The other half, or fragment, is a collection of wayward anarchistic talents responding to, and usually opposing, the society they are supposed to report.

One doesn't know whether Tomalin was writing tongue-in-cheek, but the expression of these idiosyncratic views on

British journalism earned a crisp rejoinder in the main body of the newspaper from the editorial director of Thomson Regional Newspapers who had had the opportunity of seeing the article in advance. He wrote with unveiled sarcasm of "the more coruscate talents which seem to be the needful qualifications of your 'club'."

Tomalin certainly exposed more than one Achilles heel. For example, if a journalist is going to "create interest", then surely the temptation looms to manipulate the news for that very purpose.

I don't want to give the wrong impression here. Creation of interest in the way a story is put together is a cardinal aspect of the journalist's craft. The point I am making is that, in irresponsible hands and in a competitive media situation, the facts can be dangerously distorted. But, to take the London *Sunday Times* and the other "quality" Sundays, there is no doubt that they bear out what Henry Ward Beecher said in 1887: "Nowhere else can you find so miscellaneous an amount of knowledge as is contained in a good newspaper."

On the last occasion I was in England, in 1984, I had the opportunity of recording the views of Dr Richard Clutterbuck, a former major-general in the British Army and an acknowledged authority on conflict, including terrorism. He has written extensively in this field, and I asked him about the influence of the media in the creation of a climate of violence. He gave me a long answer, and this is only one of the aspects he dealt with.

> One of the troubles is that there is an unholy marriage between the journalist and the man of violence, whether it is a violent demonstrator or a terrorist, because what a demonstrator – or for that matter usually a terrorist – tries to do is to draw attention to a point of view. And he knows that there is nothing like violence to attract attention. Now, in a society with a free press, the motivation of the journalist is to attract readers and viewers. He also knows that there is nothing comparable – apart from sex – with violence for attracting readers and viewers and lis-

teners. Therefore, there is an unholy marriage in that violence in fact – willingly or unwillingly – suits both of them, and the result is that the journalist tends to give more attention to violence, inevitably, than he does to other things, and if there is violence it will be reported. If there are ten hours of peaceful demonstration including two minutes of violence, you guess which two minutes go on the television programme.

There is no doubt at all that any sort of reporting of it inflames views and also encourages other people to imitate it when it appears on television particularly. Now to say that therefore nothing should ever be reported would be so damaging to the peaceful running of a free society as to be absolutely unacceptable. So you've got to accept that, but it's when it is irresponsibly handled by the media, that is where the blame lies.

For instance, we had some rather bad series of riots in this country in 1981, and some of the reporting, particularly the films, was done in such a way as positively to encourage people to turn out and loot. They showed almost a thing like a television commercial with a little story line, you know . . . people rather bored on the streets, and then a crash and a shop window kicked in, and then the camera zooms up on a chap putting his hand through the shop window and coming out with a tape recorder or something in it. And the only thing missing was the sort of seductive voice of a commercial . . . "Are you bored, are you fed up sitting at home. Why don't you join us?" That was the only thing missing! Those news broadcasts positively encouraged people.

When it comes to media coverage of events in South Africa, the political outlook of those involved in news reporting and dissemination can play a significant part. (See Stuart Hood's comment earlier in this chapter). Those opposed to the South African government could view their media function as a means towards overthrowing it, and so are likely to try to "make news" rather than merely to report it. The South African authorities have gone on record as saying that they have plenty of evidence of manipulation . . . not only blatant slanting of news but the stage-managing of incidents for the television cameras; Soweto pupils paid to burn school books, or encouraged to demonstrate or to commit other acts of arson. In one instance, a television crew that had arrived late persuaded bystanders to re-enact a stone-throwing incident.

But this is an old story. Years ago, at the time of Sharpeville, one of South Africa's embassies in Europe reported on filmed scenes of Blacks at Sharpeville being bombed from the air. As far as the embassy staff could determine, newsreel footage from the Spanish civil war had been slotted into the report. There were certainly no aircraft used at Sharpeville. But this again is an old trick, rehashing old footage.

More topically, the makers of the film *Mandela* which was screened on Britain's Channel 4 in September 1987 were accused of major factual errors and of creating "glamorised carboard figures". One of the critics is a former deputy-editor of the *Rand Daily Mail* (now defunct) who was known for his vigorous opposition to the South African government. He commented that the depiction of the shooting (an orderly line of policemen being given an order to fire at the crowds) differed considerably from reality. In reply, the drama controller of the television production company responsible for the film insisted that thorough research was done beforehand and that the production team had had help from "ANC people from South Africa and Tambo's son". Would one consider that an interesting admission of impartiality!

How sympathetic is the public to these machinations? In all probability much less than the media might believe. There is no doubt, as I said earlier, that the media enlarge the area of conflict.

The period of unrest through which South Africa has been passing is an example. When a general state of emergency was declared in June 1986 in order to give the authorities wider powers within which to restore order and stability to the Black areas where Black on Black violence had escalated, the media abroad tended to jump to too many conclusions which were unfounded, and to read more into "emergency" than was warranted. A London newspaper headline "South Africa in Turmoil" was a gross exaggeration of the situation. It was as if the South African media, during the riots in the London suburb of Brixton, had proclaimed "London Ablaze". Actually, it was a pity that, constitutionally, it was necessary to declare a state of emergency; "Operation Cool It" would have been more definitive and appropriate – and less emotive.

I might just interpolate something here that does not always seem to be understood. The fact that South Africa gets such extensive media coverage abroad is not only by virtue of the intrinsic interest or significance of events here but because it is a country that has had very little in the way of restrictions on visiting journalists. Comparison with other parts of the world could be illuminating.

People abroad reading reports about South Africa should be aware of the intensity of the disinformation campaign being waged against this country. There are individuals and organisations, both inside and outside the country, who know that they can count on elements of the media to help them in their efforts to discredit the South African government and the country at large. On emotional issues, of course, the process becomes much easier, as for example the Detainees' Parents' Support Committee which radiates information abroad that, on scrutiny, is found to be "false, exaggerated or distorted" (to use the words of the South African Minister of Law and Order). The retort to that is likely to be "How do you know *he* is telling the truth?" The thinking person should realise that a cabinet minister can hardly go on record with accusations of this kind without evidence to back them up, as for instance evidence of an affidavit made by a complainant only after consultation with a political activist.

On the subject of detention of children, the Minister said that, having studied the documentation and relevant information at his disposal, he had concluded that the blame for the detention of children rested squarely on the shoulders of the revolutionary activists. These people, he said, cold-bloodedly singled out children and forced them to commit cruel and disgusting deeds.

The film footage I have seen of quite young children dancing round their victims as they beat them to death and set them on fire (while still alive) beggars the imagination.

How "free" is the press? When the subject of "freedom of the press" is mentioned, it almost invariably is taken to refer to the degree of constraint imposed by the authorities. But what about the internal constraints? I had a very good acquaintance, an old newspaperman who became editor of one of South Africa's major newspapers. I liked him very much, a good man with whom to have a couple of drinks. I remember he attended a seminar on press freedom and, in answer to a question, he replied (near enough in these words) "If anyone tells me what to write, I'll tell him to get stuffed." If he had thought about it, of course, he would have realised that he was exaggerating and overlooking a very material point. Were he, as editor, to depart from the accepted policy of his newspaper group (unspoken or unwritten as it may have been), he would have received either a reprimand or his marching orders – which has happened before in this same newspaper group.

When does "press freedom" become "press licence"? Towards the end of 1985, a so-called *Freedom Fighter's Manual* was allegedly published by the American CIA for use against Nicaragua. The document detailed a number of "useful" sabotage techniques, even to the extent of describing (with diagrams) how to make an incendiary bomb, a "Molotov cocktail".

The *New Statesman* weekly in London picked this up and published extracts, substituting "Britain" for Nicaragua and called the manual "a practical guide to liberating Britain from oppression and misery by paralysing the military-industrial complex of the fascistic Thatcher state – without special tools, and at minimum personal risk for the freedom fighter". This was later reproduced in what is described as an anarchist magazine, *Red Rag*, published in Reading. The police superintendent investigating the incident was reported as saying "Special Branch investigators are examining it and our police solicitors are deciding whether there is a possible offence of incitement . . . There is enough trouble in the world without giving instructions on how to make these things and then bringing it to the notice of people who might be a little bored."

The reaction of the *New Statesman* is interesting and, to those who know the magazine, not unexpected. The then editor is reported as having said that *Red Rag* had behaved "unethically" by lifting the article without explaining that it was taken from a CIA manual. He said that he thought it was wrong of the CIA to have published the manual in the first place and that was the point his magazine was making. Which would seem, in his view, to put the *New Statesman* in the clear. However this is an old gambit – publishing questionable material coupled with an expression of disapproval . . . "Look, isn't that wicked?"

This same editor would find it instructive to turn up the files of *Punch* magazine during the editorship of Bernard Hollowood. Some twenty years ago he wrote a leading article headed "Licence to Distort". It does not point an exact parallel with the incident I have just quoted, but the "message" is as timely as ever, if not more so. This is an extract:

Those who campaign for freedom to print anything and everything do not seem aware of the appalling dangers involved. Licence to distort is harmless enough when readers are capable of recognising distortion; when readers are semi-literate and mentally off-balance, it can create a world of illusion, of imaginary evil, of ogres and fiends. Licence to distort can and does promote a licence to kill . . .

In the same way that a fine line of distinction can be drawn between recognised business practice and sharp practice, so a line can be drawn between honest, factual and unemotional reporting and what can be classed as the rabble-rousing style of journalism.

Incidentally, having mentioned the *New Statesman* weekly, I must in fairness acknowledge the change in editorial

71

approach since the new editor took over. It is no longer quite such a whingeing tract and therefore more generally informative.

My purpose in this chapter, as I said, has not been to "hammer" the media. After all, I have been part of it myself, and I think it is a great pity that the irresponsible minority foul the doorstep of the majority. My plea is for a resort to much more real information and a greater degree of rationality, perspective and honesty in viewing events in the world, and particularly – for all its faults – my own country, South Africa.

As a final thought in this chapter, I should like to point out what strikes me as a remarkable coincidence. In 1963 I was in Angola to record a radio feature on the situation there. Angola had been a Portuguese possession since 1575. In modern times it had become a province of Portugal, not a colony, and Luanda, its capital, with a population of 350 000 was the third largest Portuguese city, ranking after Lisbon and Porto. But to the world, Angola really came into the news when, in 1961, a rebellion struck the northern sector of the country. In the first three days of the attacks, along a stretch of 400 kilometres, an estimated 2 000 men, women and children of all races fell to the pangas and firearms of the rebels before troops could be rushed to the area and corps of volunteers could be organised.

As part of my fact-finding, I asked the local information office whether I could see photographs taken after the rebellion. They were most unwilling to let me see anything, saying "It's over now, we want to forget." But I asked very firmly, indicating that it was part of my job, and with great reluctance they brought out tray after tray of black-and-white photographs.

I salute them for their reluctance, but those photographs demonstrate one of the less-appreciated limitations within which the media operate. What they showed was so savage and inventively bestial that even the most elementary good taste would prohibit publication. I am similarly inhibited from describing them beyond saying that one photograph in particular – of a slaughtered Portuguese woman – was a shattering revelation of a bizarre sexual focus.

But the coincidence I wanted to mention is this. An observer wrote of the Angola affair:

> The rebellion launched one of the most remarkable propaganda drives of our times . . . I have rarely seen a campaign more beautifully timed and led by more masterly hands . . . it encompassed East and West, religious and non-religious people . . . the same arguments were used in the United Nations by representatives of the leading tyranny and the leading democracy. No wonder that the case was cut and dried and that Portugal was roundly condemned. The accused was clumsy in handling his defence. Accustomed as the Portuguese were to a happy obscurity, they did not know how to handle the storm-tossed sea of modern massive propaganda. Sometimes they remained in haughty silence, which was of course an admission of guilt. At other times they answered with arguments which only irritated an already prejudiced public opinion.

Does anyone discern a pattern recurring here, in the massive disinformation campaign that is being directed against South Africa, not least by the United Nations which spends a substantial portion of its multi-million dollar publicity allocation on radio, television and printed propaganda against South Africa?

Portugal is Western-allied, and the Portuguese provinces of Angola and Moçambique occupied long strategic coastlines on the Atlantic and Indian Oceans, as bastions of the Western alliance. Now they are in the hands of the Marxists. It is not difficult to read some significance into current events and to suspect that Western nations are being led by the nose to support growing Soviet influence in southern Africa. It should not be forgotten that this is the region referred to by Leonid Brezhnev, meaningfully as "a treasure chest". He was well aware that, between them, South Africa and the USSR (according to estimates) possess the bulk of the world's reserves of minerals such as gold, platinum, manganese, chrome and vanadium. If South Africa were to fall into the Soviet camp, there would be a Communist monopoly.

The Western world should have a very careful rethink of some of its attitudes and realise that the whipped-up emotion surrounding South Africa has gone far beyond mere opposition to apartheid. There are people who see big opportunities here to "keep the pot boiling" for further eventual gains. They are being aided by some very gullible accomplices who don't even know that they are being used.

It would be ironic if a future turn of events were to prove that the West has been in process of committing strategic suicide.

"THE POLICEMAN'S LOT IS NOT A HAPPY ONE"

(Gilbert and Sullivan)

I was strolling down the Bayswater Road in London on a summer Saturday afternoon in the early 1970's when I overtook a peaceful demonstration wending its way towards Marble Arch. There were something over a hundred, mostly young, people, and they were slouching along looking rather like a collection of unmade beds. They were being escorted by half a dozen London "bobbies" and as I fell into step with one of them, I said to him through the side of my mouth, Chicago gangster-fashion, "What would you like to do with this lot?". He was a middle-aged policeman, I took him to be one of the old school, and all he said in reply – looking scornfully at these scruffy young people – was "Oh, guv." It was said with meaning!

Those were the days before it started becoming the thing for demos to become violent; it was a pleasantly tranquil scene, with the police acting as friendly sheepdogs. I was in England in 1984 during the miners' strike and the daily television news was showing the British police with a very different face – as was the case during the inner-city riots in 1981. The question to be asked is "Has the character of the British "bobby" changed, has he become a Nazi bully as some of the more emotional arm-chair critics would suggest? Or have the circumstances changed, forcing the police into a different rôle?"

I used that quotation from Gilbert and Sullivan's *The Pirates of Penzance* to introduce this chapter because the police generally have become Aunt Sally's for anyone to pot at. They have become fair game for criticism, a lot of it ill-informed and irrational, some of it cynical and some of it

75

downright dishonest. To anyone who values objectivity and fairness, the amount of prejudiced and uninformed criticism of police activity must be disturbing. In effect, it is a wilful ignoring of what a police force is supposed to do, which is to uphold law and order irrespective of the government in power. Emotion runs away with good sense.

The South African Police, of course, come into this picture, but I am talking in general terms, having discussed this subject with senior police officers in the United Kingdom and in the United States of America. Take a simple case by way of illustration. There is a demo on the go. Television cameras are present, very often having been alerted in advance by the demo organisers. An "incident" happens when someone hurls a brick at a policeman. Television cameras are not quick enough to film the initial provocation, but home in just in time to film the policeman reacting. This is immediately taken in some circles to be "unprovoked police brutality". I would add a corollary; in the unrest that South Africa has been experiencing in the Black townships, although there are numerically almost as many non-White as White police, and they operate largely in unison, foreign television news teams seemed all too often to film only White policemen in action, for reasons which will be obvious.

On the subject of numerical strengths, when I was in the USA in 1976, I was told by a spokesman at police headquarters in New York that the city's police establishment was of the order of 30 000, but at the time the force was down to around 26 000 through problems with the city's finances. In Chicago, I was told that the city's police establishment was approxmately 33 000.

It is significant to note the following figures for the South African Police which, by comparison, makes them remarkably "thin on the ground" compared with many other countries.

S.A.P. establishment end of 1960	White	11 938
	Non-White	13 786
S.A.P. establishment end of 1970	White	16 346
	Non-White	15 531

S.A.P. establishment end of 1981	White	17 303
	Non-White	16 968
S.A.P. establishment June 1986	White	26 463
	Non-White	22 458

So what price the expression "police state" which is levelled at South Africa? It is usually trotted out if the police knock on a suspect's door in the night hours. What do police forces in other parts of the world do – send the suspect a postcard asking him to report to the nearest police station? If South Africa were a "police state", would thousands of Blacks from neighbouring states cross its borders illegally to work in South Africa?

Torture at the hands of the police is one of the constantly repeated allegations against South Africa. But despite all the facile talk, how many people base their allegations on actual fact? I don't say it doesn't happen, but I would make two reservations. The first is that "torture" is a very relative term. To some, the mildest of persuasion will rank as torture – and elements of the media, often without proof, will be only too ready to blow up the allegation to sensational heights.

The second reservation is to ask how many countries in the world can truthfully claim that their police forces have never indulged in "torture" – again accepting that torture is a relative term.

Here again, emotional reaction allows rationality to fly out the window. Consider the following example of the sort of thing that has been happening in South Africa. A person is arrested on suspicion of having smuggled arms and explosives into South Africa and having cached them for the purpose of a future terrorist attack aimed almost invariably at a soft target, such as a crowded shopping centre, with women and children the most likely victims. Many innocent people have already been killed. The police have to find out urgently (before an attack can take place) where the arms and explosives are hidden. What approach must they take? Do they say "Excuse me sir, but when you have a moment, would you be so good as to tell us something about the arms cache?"

The incidence of strong-arm methods is certainly not confined to South Africa. Ask around in the United Kingdom (Northern Ireland would be a fruitful field of inquiry) and the United States of America, quite apart from the multitude of countries which seem to incur little or no opprobrium for their suspect activities.

The Biko case was overtly shameful but not unique ... and this is not to play down that tragic incident. Even the record of the British police and prison authorities is marred from time to time with reports of deaths in detention and failure to provide medical attention.

In February 1987, there was a headline in a local newspaper "Aussie 'killer cops' race row". It concerned allegations that Aborigines have been kicked and beaten to death by White policemen and jail warders. Subsequently (August 1987) it was reported that the Australian Minister of Aboriginal Affairs had launched a high-level investigation, 16 Aborigines having died in prison in the previous eight months. The newspaper, *The Australian*, said in a lead story that similar circumstances in South Africa would have led to unparalleled protest from the international community, including the Australian government. As indeed would have been the case had it been South Africa, and not France, that had deported 101 illegal Black immigrants in chains. According to newspaper reports, they were chained at the wrist and ankle and were taken to Orly airport bound for Mali. Heavily armed police escorted them aboard and, in some cases, chained them to their seats.

On the subject of Biko, doubts were expressed in South Africa by two of his closest Black friends, in advance of the release of the Attenborough film on the life and death of Steve Biko. The Johannesburg *Sunday Times* reported one of them as "slamming" the book *Asking for Trouble* by Donald Woods, on which the multi-million dollar film is based, as "more a romantic ego trip than it can ever be historically and politically precise". Woods, a former newspaper editor, is described as "a nice white guy but also a very gullible liberal ... over and above the false stories about Woods having to swim across crocodile-infested waters to freedom, I see the film and the emphasis it is alleged to portray as a personal attempt by Attenborough to exploit a possibly very gullible market." Another friend believes the film appears set to exploit the "brief" and "superficial" relationship between Woods and Biko.

Another question to be asked is to what extent is the individual's perception of the police coloured by the selectivity of media presentation? Another question; how many of those who criticise have ever been exposed to situations in which, of routine, police find themselves, when life or death decisions have to be made in split seconds?

The notorious Sharpeville incident is a case in point. How many people know (I would bet not one in a million who know the name Sharpeville) that only two months earlier nine members of the South African Police were set upon and murdered by a Black mob in Cato Manor, Natal. So when a comparatively small force of police was surrounded by thousands of protesters at Sharpeville police station, with the surrounding wire fence likely to give way with the weight of bodies pressing against it, what would the feelings of the average person have been? It was ostensibly a "peaceful" protest, but if you know anything of Africa you will know that a mob can turn savage at the drop of a hat, particularly when you have ululating women in the background egging the men on. Some details of the incident still appear to be clouded, but someone must have given the order to fire or else a nervous finger let off a shot and that became the signal for a volley. These things can happen as any soldier will tell you. It was a tragic incident, but not unique.

The world now recognises a Sharpeville Day. What about an Amritsar Day to commemorate the 379 men, women and children killed and the approximately 1 200 wounded when troops under Brigadier R E H Dyer opened fire, reportedly without warning, on a mass meeting in the Indian city of Amritsar in 1919? Of course, for South Africans, the question "Why is there not an Amritsar Day recognised round the world?" is purely rhetorical. We are well accustomed to the selective indignation directed at us. For the record, the gathering at Amritsar was reported to have been peaceful, but that General Dyer considered his troops to have been threatened. Of course, to this day Amritsar remains a trouble spot with continuing loss of life there.

On the subject of Sharpeville, an interesting sidelight on the reformist mood in South Africa at the present time was the conferring on State President Botha in June 1987 of the Freedom of Lekoa, a Black urban complex encompassing six Black towns, one of which is Sharpeville. The ceremony was conducted by the Black mayor of Lekoa.

Now I come to armchair sophistry. First of all, where is the moral outrage when police are killed while carrying out their duties? The so-called "victims" of police action are often lauded as martyrs, but when a policeman dies upholding law and order, or protecting lives and property, that is regarded as his job. When a policeman is provoked or threatened, what must his reaction be? If someone comes at him with a firearm or a petrol bomb (or even a stone, which can be lethal), is he expected to stand fast and not react "because he is trained"? I have had that argument put forward by an armchair critic … "Oh, but he is trained." Put that argument to the dead policeman's widow and family.

Black policemen, of course, have been prime targets during the unrest in the Black townships, the aim being to murder them as "collaborators in the system". Many have been killed in a most gruesome way, in the majority of instances while the policeman was off duty. More than 800 homes of Black policemen have been destroyed. It is a shocking commentary on the methods of the activists that in a number of cases the graves of murdered policemen have been desecrated; the bodies have been dug up and then set alight in public.

Some clergymen who are in the forefront of the "liberation struggle" might well search their souls and consciences as to whether they have not compromised themselves by their apparent silence in the matter of the Biblical commandment "Thou shalt not kill".

There is no doubt of the involvement of the African National Congress. One of their spokesmen said at California State University in October 1985: "We want to make the death of a collaborator so grotesque that the people will never think of it."

It has been reported that the South African police authorities were highly disturbed over the lack of emphasis which local and international news media were giving to the "shocking violence" being perpetrated against Blacks in the townships by mobs. Innumerable Black homes have been burnt down without regard for the men, women or children inside them. A senior police spokesman said "There is only one purpose behind this wanton violence of Black against Black – that is to intimidate the ordinary, decent, law-abiding people into joining the mobs bent on destroying order in the townships."

The South African Police, of course, are doing their best to preserve law and order and to save lives, but because of their comparatively small number (refer back to the details given earlier which reveal that the SAP's strength is considerably less than the police forces of two major American cities), troops had to be called in to help patrol. Yet the cry goes out "Get the troops out of the townships, they are only a provocation." This is about as logical as saying "Get the troops out of Northern Ireland, they are only a provocation." It seems not to be realised that the basics of good policing is to prevent unlawful behaviour rather than having to take action once such behaviour has taken place.

In this context, it was sad to find Archbishop Tutu, Nobel Peace Prize winner, reported as saying "As a Black person I know we don't regard the police as our friends. No, let me put it strongly. We regard the police as our enemies." On the evidence, however, he certainly does not speak for the majority of the Black population who are only too thankful to have the presence of the forces of law and order. In fact, in certain instances, "clean up" operations in the townships are at the behest of the local Black community. A poll conducted in mid-1987 in the town of Alexandra outside Johannesburg found that 92 per cent of residents were in favour of having security forces in the town.

It has been conceded at top level in the Police that, in a situation of widespread unrest where members of the security forces are day and night involved in confrontation with violent mobs, there will be instances in which members of the force overstep the mark in dealing with the perpetrators. An interesting dichotomy in public attitudes to the police arises here. On the one hand, their critics say that the police are using "inhuman methods", but if a policeman should react in a normal human way to an attacker who is trying to kill or maim him, then he is slated. And even juveniles, about whose detention there has been an outcry, can be just as lethal with a weapon, whether a brick or a petrol bomb, or a gun, as any adult. It should go without saying that in disturbed conditions, the public have an obligation to indulge in more clear thinking and less emotion.

I am reminded of a long conversation I had with the best-selling American author James A Michener when he was in South Africa some years ago. This was shortly after his book on the tragic incident at Kent State University in Ohio appeared. To recap briefly, there was unrest on the campus and the National Guard was called in to help the police. The Guard was subjected to a great amount of provocation by way of taunting and abuse and eventually they fired a volley and four students were killed. I taped this conversation with Mr Michener, and I am quoting from it to illustrate what provocation can, in certain circumstances, lead to.

The Guard were not menaced in any conceivable way by any conceivable number of students. You know, the four students killed were of the order of two football fields away from the men who fired the rifles. The men who fired the rifles could hardly have known whether the person they were firing at – I don't believe they were firing at anybody, but if they had been – they couldn't even tell whether it was a boy or girl, they were so far away.

But the cause was not what the Guards said. I think the cause was natural panic and maybe forgivable panic on the part of the very young soldiers, many of them college students themselves. One of the men who we know fired more bullets than anybody else was himself a student. So I think it was a tragedy, accidental. I don't think there was collusion leading to it. I think it was a bunch of men under duress who said "Well, if they give us any more trouble, we'll let them have it" ...

In the book I point out that one of the precipitating factors in the tragedy was the foul language used by the students against the Guard and against the police, and particularly by the girl students. Now a lot of people have said "Well, Mr Michener, you're an idiot to think that foul language has any effect, they were just saying things, and nobody has a right to get mad at that." This I cannot accept. I think that language is a weapon in social affairs, and to abuse it wantonly is to invite disaster. I can only say that at Kent there is adequate evidence both in tape recording and the verbal reports of the people involved that the language was just unbelievably bad, and particularly on the part of the girl students, and that this so repelled the forces of law and order to hear a college student using language like this – many of them having wanted to go to college themselves and failed, or wanting their children to go at great expense – that they were both bewildered by it and repelled by it, and that their animosity towards the students was therefore increased.

I find this also in many aspects of our present agitation. People are saying things that are quite excessive. I can think of phrases that I might throw at you and you would have the right to punch me in the nose, it's as simple as that. Words are not idle, words are not meaningless; they do carry overtones of tremendous freight and, if abused, will have consequences.

It is a truism to say that, to some extent, the police are there to be provoked. If they have to enforce laws with which some people disagree – particularly when it comes to politics – then these same people are likely to turn their frustrations upon the police. The net effect is that the police are then regarded as outside the common society.

I came upon this phenomenon during a period of student unrest when I happened to be broadcasting a series of opinions features which were immediately dubbed "controversial".

There was the most vituperative and intemperate criticism of the police at large, so much so that I went on the air saying words to the effect "Hey, wait a minute; who are we talking about? Some invasion of foreigners? These are our own South African young men; they are part of our society; they are the ones you ask for help when you have a problem ... they are us." I know full well that this sort of attitude does not go down well in certain circles here in South Africa in which it is fashionable (almost on principle) to decry the police force which is largely composed of Afrikaners. For the most part, the English-speaking section don't fancy the job, so it is a facile ploy to cast aspersions. Be that as it may, one of the most warming moments I have ever had in radio was when the telephone rang after that broadcast and a woman's voice said "I am a policeman's wife, I just want to say thank you for what you said".

On my last visit to Britain in 1984, I had the chance of talking at some length to a very distinguished policeman, a former Commissioner of London's Metropolitan Police, Sir Robert Mark. Over the years he had worked up a very good relationship with the media, and it was his feeling that for every journalist who interprets a situation unfairly, there is another who is perfectly anxious to put it right. Among South Africa's multi-lingual press, that situation does not exist. The bulk of the English-language press is anti-government and will not necessarily be too anxious "to put it right". There are not infrequent instances of unsubstantiated allegations against the police being published in newspapers (some of them palpably from unreliable sources) and although there might subsequently be a watering down of the allegation by the newspaper (though seldom a denial), the build-up of this sort of criticism cannot but have a damaging effect on police morale and public confidence.

If one turns the spotlight away from South Africa, these extracts from advertisements published in 1986 make interesting reading.

The new Public Order Bill plans to give the police new powers to control and prevent the right to protest. If the Bill becomes law, and it probably will do, the police will be able to control and dictate the terms on which this right may be exercised. The organisers of a march will have to give six clear days notice of it to the police. The Bill will create new police powers to impose conditions on your protest in advance or on the spot – for a wide range of reasons. The police will have new powers of arrest and it will be a criminal offence not to abide by their conditions. The Bill also creates other new offences, including one of 'disorderly conduct' and others of riot, violent disorder and affray.

The Police Bill of 1984 is now the Police and Criminal Evidence Act. As of 1st January this year, it is fully operational. It marks a new level of police powers. It allows the police to decide what arrestable offences are 'serious' and to use 'reasonable' force in the exercise of their new powers.

The police now have extended powers to stop and search you. And they have new powers to establish road blocks and search premises. They can arrest you for any offence if, for example, you fail to give your name and address. The police can also detain you at a police station without contact with the outside world for up to 36 hours. They can strip-search you and submit you to an intimate body search.

Is this the coming into being of a new "police state"? I hardly think so. The two advertisements were published in the left-wing *New Statesman* in London and emanated from the (now defunct) Greater London Council which offered further information to the public on these new departures. The reasonable person would probably interpret them as indicating a realistic adaptation on the part of the authorities to changed circumstances in Britain when its police forces can no longer afford to be the "friendly sheep-dogs" pictured at the start of this chapter.

Perhaps significantly, the edition of the *New Statesman* in which these advertisements appeared had on its cover a photograph of massed police with the caption "Their law, their order". It would seem to reinforce what I was suggesting ... to regard the police as outsiders in the common society, "them" and not "us".

A final thought on the subject of the "police state", that evocative and emotional and loosely applied term. If South Africa had been a police state and its prime minister had been assassinated while sitting in his place in Parliament, what would have been the fate of the assassin? Surely he would have been summarily executed. This is the actual case of Dr H F Verwoerd who was stabbed to death by a parliamentary messenger. The assassin was brought to trial, but the Supreme Court judge (an Afrikaner, by the way) took no time at all to decide that the accused was mentally not fit to be tried for murder, and he was confined to a mental institution.

By way of postscript ... the story is told of the police constable on a lonely beat coming upon a woman in labour. There is nobody to help, so he does what he can and delivers the baby, which he then holds up by the heels (which he believes is the correct routine) and gives it a smack on the bottom. Whereupon the baby snarls "Police brutality".

STUDENT PROTEST

Education is learning what you didn't even know you didn't know.
(Historian Daniel Boorstin.)

In the 1960's, when I was Organiser of the English Radio Service in Cape Town, I had a call from the then President of the National Union of South African Students, one Adrian Leftwich. The visit was in connection with a student programme that was running weekly on the Afrikaans Service (dealing with student activities generally) and he was concerned that there was no equivalent for the English-language universities. He implied that this was another example of discrimination against the English-speaking section.

I assured him that this was not the case; the only reason that there was no such programme on the English Radio Service was that we wanted first to be satisfied that there would be an adequacy of good material countrywide to sustain a weekly half-hour. I said that NUSAS, being a national organisation, was in the ideal position to act as a co-ordinating body to ensure the cooperation of all universities in the interests of giving the student body at large a platform. I invited Mr Leftwich to discuss the matter with the members of his organisation and come up with some firm ideas. I assured him that the South African Broadcasting Corporation was only too keen to have a student programme but that I, as the person who would be responsible for it, was not prepared to start something that might soon fold because of lack of sustained support.

That was the last I heard from him. Apparently the idea of getting involved in a programme of that kind was too tame. NUSAS already had its sights on bigger things, to wit political involvement, on an anti-government stance, and as a consequence of his activities in this sphere, Adrian Leftwich eventually skipped the country.

87

The whole story of student activism in the 1960's and 1970's, with some spill-over in present times, is fresh in the memory of many people, but many questions remain. How does student unrest so often escalate? Without doubt the media, willy nilly, enlarge the area of dispute or conflict. It's fun if you're a youngster and you find the media flatteringly attentive to your views. And demonstrations can be fun, too, whether you really know what you're demonstrating about, or don't really care. Demos are unprogrammed activities in a highly organised society and, judging by the faces one sees on the television screen, many of the participants are enjoying the affair, until the violence starts.

I was recording radio programmes in the United States of America, in the aftermath of the student unrest there, and I sought out Professor John Searle, Professor of Philosophy on the Berkeley campus of the University of California, seed-bed of the student unrest – one could call it revolt. He is the author of a Pelican paperback *The Campus War*, subtitled *a sympathetic look at the university in agony*. Professor Searle, incidentally, is a former American Rhodes Scholar and received a B.A. in philosophy, politics and economics and a D.Phil at Christ Church, Oxford where for three years he was a philosophy don while completing his doctorate. He is also a recent BBC Reith Lecturer. John Searle's book is written from a liberal standpoint, and he was originally one of the faculty leaders in the free speech movement at Berkeley. But then his outlook changed, and he told me why.

When I first got interested in these matters was in the great days of the civil rights movement in the Martin Luther King era. In those days there was non-violence and a concern for civil liberties and civil rights, and I was active in that portion. But then as the Vietnam war developed, there was a radical change in the behaviour of the student movement. They became much more violent; the leadership tended to pass into the hands of people who were much more extremist and radical, and indeed, in many cases, self-described revolutionaries, and at that point I began to fight those trends in the student movement. Now obviously if you have been siding with a movement and then the movement changes and you start fighting against it, people are bound to say well, you've changed. But in fact, it did not seem to me that I had changed; it seemed to me that the student radical movement had changed from being a very sensible non-violent civil libertarian organisation or movement to being a radical, violent revolutionary – and I felt totalitarian – movement. At that point I began to fight it with everything I had.

This is perhaps a lesson that needs to be absorbed. John Searle, I am sure, would be proud to describe himself as a liberal. But that did not stop him from opposing strongly what he considered illiberal tendencies.

I earned myself a considerable amount of opprobrium some years ago in so-called "liberal" circles when there was a lot of student unrest in Cape Town and elsewhere in South Africa. I went on the air with some alternative points of view to those being peddled by, among others, the bulk of the English-language press which was uniformly anti-government in its utterances. It so happened that I was halfway through a series of weekly half-hour programmes (which I may say were my idea, not inspired by the SABC) when there was an incident in the centre of Cape Town. White students protesting about the inferiority of what was then referred to as Bantu education (we have since dropped the word Bantu in favour of Black) were rousted by police off the steps of the Anglican cathedral which is fairly close to the Houses of Parliament. I won't go into all the details (some of which are in any case clouded and subject to highly partisan opinion); suffice to say the incident raised a storm in South Africa and there was great argument as to whether the students had been warned to disperse, whether it was a set-up job to teach the students a lesson, and whether the police had used excessive force – certainly no firearms were used.

Be that as it may, I had the temerity (according to critics) to go on the air suggesting that whereas protest marches and slogans are one thing, the practical implications of the protest (almost invariably ignored) are quite another. I put forward the thought that people might have been more impressed with the genuineness of the protest if students had held up placards reading "We demand increased income tax to pay for better education for non-Whites", or "Reduce White university subsidies to educate Black children". There was also a niggling thought that the students, while some of them were genuinely committed to the protest, were being put up as Aunt Sally's by an over-encouraging press and by adults who were not prepared to "stand up and be counted" and who were seeing this as an opportunity to work off some of their own political frustrations. To say this sort of thing immediately put me in the enemy camp, and I remember an "open letter" written by a group of students to a local newspaper expressing their disappointment that someone who had seemed to them to be a decent and popular broadcaster had somehow shown a cloven hoof.

The unwillingness to hear another viewpoint persists to this day and from time to time you find speakers invited onto a campus being shouted down, surely a negation of what a university stands for. It is perhaps summed up by a girl student who, on being offered an alternative way of looking at things by a professor friend of mine, protested "You mustn't do that; you're brainwashing me".

In that "offending" broadcast of mine I also wondered whether we have been unfair to students in assuming that they have more to contribute to our affairs than is the actual case. Nobody denies them their idealism and their vigour and their enthusiasm, but nobody has a monopoly of wisdom and perception and compassion and concern. "We shouldn't regard them", I said, "as belonging to some special sort of trade union in this respect." Anybody can stand up and declaim "this is wrong." But it's like being angry. Remember the words of Aristotle?

> Anybody can be angry, that is easy. But to be angry with the right person, and to the right degree, and at the right time, and for the right purpose, and in the right way – that is not easy.

Furthermore – and this may sound harsh to young people

and to some older ones, too – if students want to provoke a confrontation with the authorities, then they must be prepared to accept the consequences and not squeal. They should abide by the Harry S Truman dictum to the effect that if you can't stand the heat, get out of the kitchen. They should realise that once an "incident" is sparked off, innocent bystanders can willy nilly become involved.

I am too old to accept that some young person with a gift for jargon is an "intellectual". In 1970, I was in the United Kingdom preparing a series of radio features and I had occasion to visit the University of Sussex near Brighton to record a couple of speakers there. It was just after the Indian High Commissioner had been invited to deliver the Kingsley Memorial Lecture but was shouted down by the students of the University. It so happened that I was sold a copy of *English Student* by an earnest young woman. It was a broadsheet describing itself as the official organ of the English Student Movement, and in it I read with fascination the grounds on which the guest speaker was denied a hearing. I quote verbatim:

> ... he comes from a petty warlord family, which has been a servile tool of the Indian compradour bureaucrat capitalist government and a servile tool of U.S. imperialism and Soviet Social imperialism and that he received a British bourgeois education in Cambridge.

I found it difficult to find a way through this turgid nonsense. The United States and the Soviet Union both take a knock, and the only person who might emerge with some satisfaction is an Oxford man! Truly Alexander Pope was right when he said that "a little learning is a dang'rous thing". And, in more modern (and cinematic) times, there is the quirkish remark by the Chinese detective Charlie Chan in one of those delightful old movies: "Mind, like parachute, only work when open".

A recent example of student intolerance and abuse of the intellect took place at the University of Cape Town in October 1986. Dr Conor Cruise O'Brien, Irish academic and writer and a former Irish Foreign Minister, had been invited by the Political Science Department of the University to give a series of lectures on societies in a state of siege – this in defiance of an academic boycott of South Africa that had been promoted abroad. Dr O'Brien's "liberal" credentials are impeccable; he is a former chairman of the Irish Anti-apartheid Movement and, among other things, a former editor-in-chief of the London *Observer* newspaper. What is more, he has two adopted Black children.

But, notwithstanding, his first two lectures were disrupted by militant students who broke into the lecture rooms, with a degree of violence, and this led to the cancellation of the remainder of the course of lectures because of the threat of further violence. Dr O'Brien said that the students' actions held serious implications and he was concerned at the threat posed to academic freedom. To quote him further: "Under a false banner of anti-apartheid, militant students are trying to take over and dictate who should speak". This was a vital threat to academic freedom, he said, and an academic boycott posed the threat of wrecking South African universities which were of "critical importance" to a future non-racial South Africa. He said that universities are about communication and freedom of intellectual communication, hence his opposition to an academic boycott. The sad thing is that the University of Cape Town, as with other "White" universities, has long had an "open" (i.e. non-racial) admission policy, and has a consistent record of opposition to apartheid. The campaign of disruption (to protest against Dr O'Brien's "betrayal" of the boycott) was led by a student organisation the majority of whose members are Black. There was similar disruption at the University of the Witwatersrand in Johannesburg, another university in the forefront of the "liberal struggle".

If anyone finds lack of logic in the attitude of these Black students, he is quite right, but it is an aspect of the so-called "politics of refusal" which takes in such concepts as "no enlightenment before liberation". In the same way, Black schoolchildren have been manipulated to proclaim "no education before liberation" ... if not in these actual words, at least in action.

However, one of the most disturbing elements in the whole sorry business as affecting Dr O'Brien's visit was that apparently more than eighty staff members of the University of Cape Town allied themselves with the disruption. In the minds of many people they would seem to have forfeited their right to the word "university". The ability to separate the emotions from the intellect must surely be a major responsibility on the part of members of a "university".

There was a considerable amount of public reaction against the student actions as well as the attitude of these staff members. This attitude was put into words by the Chairwoman of the University of Cape Town Academic Staff Association who said (according to a published report) "The University's rôle is not to provide a platform for all shades of opinion but rather to decide what will count as knowledge and to exclude what does not ... unless Black students see academic freedom being used to contribute towards a better, more democratic society, they will see it as continuing protection of the White minority".

One wonders whether this chairwoman is old enough to know anything about Adolph Hitler and his regime. Perhaps a burning on campus of non-approved books is now on the cards at UCT.

People who "pay the piper" as far as university financing is concerned (and what a costly investment universities are) should take the trouble to satisfy themselves that they are getting value for money when it comes to such aspects as the intellectual obligations vested in universities. I believe that a much more critical spotlight should be directed at attitudes and statements that, by default, gain credence and get well on the way towards becoming accepted norms. As Bryan Wilson said in his book *The Youth Culture and the Universities:*

> While a university obviously has a responsibility to encourage critical thinking about existing social and other institutions, it is not its task to pass on emotionally hostile orientations in the guise of scholarly criticism.

While one can up to a point understand the feeling on the

part of some Blacks that "universities represent powerful interest groups striving to preserve the status quo and are not relevant to a changing South Africa", it is a perilous concept to envisage that what has been built up over centuries should carelessly be ditched. Abolishing one culture is a drastic way of eliminating a culture gap, but one should be aware that there are people who would not be unhappy to see the baby thrown out with the bathwater. And we need to be on our guard against misinterpreting the rôle of a university as against, say, a Technikon – which has a great deal of "relevance" in a Third World situation.

With as much sympathy as one can muster for some of the manifest difficulties with which Black students have had – and still have – to contend, it is very hard to justify the incident in April 1987 at Rhodes University in Grahamstown when students protesting about alleged racist practices in the allocation of bursaries ran wild and caused damage after a sit-in in the Administration block. A University spokesman made it clear that in 1986 Black students received 43 per cent of the bursaries while representing only 22 per cent of the student body.

The sadness is that, in siding with radical students, staff members are doing the student body a disservice. No taxpayer takes kindly to supporting that kind of behaviour at universities. There is a mistaken belief among their supporters that activist students are pursuing a liberal line. This is very often not so; their attitudes and activities are often far from "liberal", and some of these students could turn, at the drop of a hat, into nasty little totalitarians.

Subsequently there was disruption again at the University of Cape Town when about 150 Black students forced Dr Denis Worrall to abandon his after-dinner speech as the guest of one of the University residences. Dr Worrall is a former member of the National Party and former South African Ambassador in London who left the National Party to stand as an independent candidate in the last election. There was also an assault on a Black "moderate" who had been invited to speak on campus. Twenty per cent of the

94

student body at UCT is Black, and the attitude of the radicals among them can hardly be interpreted otherwise than as "We don't care a damn about your traditional university values and we are not prepared to adapt to them. We demand a 'people's university' where we will hear, and be taught, what we want."

There has been a growing feeling among the public that university authorities have been too "soft" with the radical element. One can appreciate their predicament in not wanting to create the circumstances for violence on campus and, perhaps as much as anything, not wanting to risk the appearance of being "racist". But this attitude is judged as appeasement with all its doubtful benefits. However, this latest example of illiberal radicalism and intolerance at last moved the UCT authorities to take disciplinary action in the way of rustication of some students and monetary fines on others. The realisation may grow that, in their disruption of university activities, radical students (themselves a minority) are using freedom to destroy freedom.

Encouragement by faculty members, tacit or otherwise, of student protest and violence seems to have been a common feature of the unrest on United States campuses in the 1960's. One of the less admirable aspects, which was deplored in some quarters at the time, was the giving in by university authorities to unreasonable student demands. "No police on campus" was by way of being uncontestable to many student activists. Someone with whom that didn't wash was Dr S I Hayakawa, President of San Francisco State University. He later became a United States Senator, but when I met him he had just retired from the University and was acting in an advisory capacity. I reminded him of the occasion, widely reported at the time, when he committed the heresy of calling the police onto his campus when students appeared bent on arson. This is what he said to me in a long recorded interview.

A remarkable number of professors – and prestigious professors in great universities – still hold it against me that I called the police – and the general public were all in favour of it, including graduates of the University of even five or ten years ago. Some of our activists and dissident professors here were completely shocked at the reaction of their own friends and relatives outside the University at the tremendous support I was getting. Now I was simply doing the commonsense thing, but for some reason or other, I was suddenly the villain to a large number of intellectuals.

You see, I'm a devout believer in academic freedom, and ever since the victory of the Free Speech movement at the University of California at Berkeley – that was in 1964 – ever since then academic freedom has been diminishing. That is, from that moment on, students felt it quite alright to disrupt the classroom and shout obscenities at the professor and say that what he is speaking is nonsense, or that his courses are irrelevant to the problems of our time. Then, of course, we had the enormous phenomenon of none being able to defend President Johnson's policies on Vietnam on the campus without being hooted at, or having tomatoes – furniture – thrown at him and so on. Steadily there was a diminution of academic freedom.

Also, there was the outburst of violence all over the place – acts of arson, acts of intimidation and so on, and the outright use of explosives on campus. Well, it seems to me that the calling in of the police, which I did, is nothing extraordinary, not requiring great original thinking. If you were running an hotel, or an airport, or a department store, and people were starting to commit arson and beat up the customers, you have to call the police.

Now there was a most extraordinary reaction to this. In the next room – now that I have finished my presidency I've finally got time to do it – I have half a room full of big cartons full of telegrams and letters that came to me after I became president, fan mail, and let's say for every stack a yard tall of letters supporting my position, there was about half an inch opposing it. Now these letters do not come from conservatives, necessarily, or liberals; they come from everybody. They came from schoolteachers, they came from businessmen, they came from political clubs, they came from chambers of commerce, and all over the State and in other states, too. There was a kind of thing saying "It's about time someone called the police to throw those apes off the campus" ... they used words like apes to describe the students. The most touching letters came from people who had never been to university themselves. They said "I was too poor to get to university, my mother was sick and I had to support her, and I couldn't go to university." And here, in their eyes, students who had the privilege of going to university were tearing it up. They were completely baffled and bewildered. They said "Call the police, call the National Guard, call anybody you like." This was a quite amazing phenomenon. At dry-cleaning shops and drug stores and hotel lobbies and little corner grocery stores, people put out pads of paper on top of which were the words "We love you, Dr. Hayakawa", and there was space underneath for people to sign their names. People would send me from various towns all over California pads of these papers, and I would say that we got a cross-section in my support of the entire spectrum of political opinions and occupational levels.

I want to make it absolutely clear that in no sense am I using quotes from interviews I conducted in the United States to reinforce any arguments I may put forward in respect of the situation in South Africa, then or now. The brief I gave myself in recording these interviews was to seek views on the American scene from Americans themselves, and in no way to seek to make comparisons or to score points. The people who were kind enough to give me their time spoke to me in good faith on this basis which I had explained to them beforehand.

Reverting to those "controversial" broadcasts of mine, I was receiving so much correspondence that I set down my thoughts on a separate sheet of paper to be attached to my reply so that they would not have to be typed over and over again. Here they are:

I think we can agree that it is easy to enjoy the comfort of opinion without the discomfort of thought.

Prejudice is a great time-saver; it enables one to form or hold opinions without having to worry about facts.

Often we subject facts to a prefabricated set of interpretations.

We are irritated, and sometimes furious, to be given facts which clash with, or demolish, long and fondly-held convictions, and we tend to protest in these circumstances that we are being brainwashed.

When we say "I am very open-minded", we usually mean "I am receptive to my own preconceived ideas, prejudices and fears".

We are not half as ready to hear the other man's point of view as we would like to think. Thereby we are subscribing to a form of intellectual "apartheid".

When we are fed information and opinion which differs from what we normally take in from our accustomed sources (such as the newspapers we read which themselves are subjectively chosen), we tend to react – as with indigestion – noisily.

Here it is pertinent, I think, to quote something written by Arthur M. Schlesinger Jr in his book *The Crisis of Confidence* subtitled *ideas, power and violence in America* (Andre Deutsch, London). Schlesinger, as some will remember, was a special assistant to President John F Kennedy and subsequently wrote the best-selling *A Thousand Days* dealing with that presidential term, which netted him the Pulitzer Prize for Biography in 1966. At the time I met him, he was (and still is, as far as I know) Albert Schweitzer Professor of the Humanities at the City University of New York. His office was on the 16th floor of the Graduate Centre, and I remember the magnificent view of the Empire State Building a few blocks away.

The Crisis of Confidence was published in 1969 and dealt with the turbulence of the times in the United States. Certain passages would seem to me to have a universal and all-time application.

Ideas are the means by which a rational society comes to terms with a changing environment. The turbulent and unpredictable world in which we live makes good ideas – ideas which comprehend the present and anticipate the future – more indispensable than ever. But ideas to exert power must bear some relation to actuality. Intellectuals too often rush into public affairs armed only with emotion and ignorance. If they really wish to shape events, they must join the expertise of the intellectual technician with the passion and general creativity of the man of general ideas. They will influence government most effectively not by learning the art of public relations, not by turning themselves into publicists or hucksters, not by organising pressure groups and marches on Washington, but by thinking hard about basic problems and coming up with basic answers ...

Reason without passion is sterile; passion without reason is hysterical; and the two must be united in effective public action. If the man of ideas remains faithful to his vocation – which is neither automatic obeisance nor automatic hostility to power but the disciplined and, if need be, passionate use of reason in pursuit of understanding – he need not fear his capacity to live and move in the world of power. But if intellectuals themselves conspire to destroy the discipline of reason, if they help turn our politics into a competition in unreason and fanaticism, we reduce the chance of solving any of our problems and abandon our society to those most skilled and ruthless in the use of force.

There is an old-fashioned expression that I have not encountered for years that applies to some current university attitudes and that is *trahison des clercs* ... literally, the treason of learned men, otherwise defined as the betrayal of intellectual obligations. It is an expression that might well be resurrected.

And someone should produce a crisp and unequivocal

definition of academic freedom to disabuse the minds of some undergraduates that it provides carte blanche during their university years to throw stones and create disturbances. This definition could well be adopted as a motto for every university and displayed prominently.

I must tell a couple of stories against myself, apropos the flak I was getting from students and others. In the Radio Review column of a local newspaper appeared this paragraph.

Much as I disliked Dewar McCormack's programme *Encounter* last week, its potentially dangerous influence was happily minimised by the fact that it was so utterly boring – and Mr. McCormack's presentation must take at least some of the credit for that.

I was intrigued to note that the comment was written by a young man whom I had failed at an announcer's audition not long before. Inter alia, I might just mention that this particular newspaper reviewed (unfavourably, of course) a programme that had never been broadcast – it was cancelled at the last minute.

But judging from published comment, I had become something of a dangerous subversive. One reference was headed "SABC Propaganda for Intellectuals"

Until recently the S.A.B.C.'s main propaganda programme has been *Current Affairs,* but its shortcoming is that it is pitched too low. It caters for the non intellectual masses. Listeners with a higher I.Q. treat it as a joke.

Now a new propaganda programme has been introduced, pitched for more intelligent listeners. It is Mr Dewar McCormack's *Encounter* programme. It serves up the same old Nationalist propaganda but it sets about it more subtly. It is more sophisticated.

A reader submitted a verse parody which was also published.

To Dewar McCormack (with apologies to Ogden Nash)

How courteous, like the Japanese
He always says "Excuse me, please!"

100

Moves step by step into your garden
With smiles and with "I beg your pardon!"
A subtle slant, a snide relay,
And always in the chummiest way
Assuring us with hand on heart
There is no malice in his dart –
Mere summing up of what is said
To keep us all from going Red.
He bows and grins a friendly grin,
Creeping a little further in,
Then grins and bows a friendly bow,
"Dear students, this is my garden now!"

I must say I rather liked that parody. I subsequently met its author and we had a good laugh together and actually became rather "chummy", to use the word in her parody.

I hope that nothing that has been said in this chapter will be taken as reflecting disparagingly on students generally. But rationality can all too easily become a casualty of student enthusiasm and lead them into attitudes and actions that are not in the best interests of the student body at large. Bloody-mindedness can all too easily alienate public sympathy, particularly when there is a suspicion that students are being manipulated for less than idealistic motives. And students should not forget that the taxes paid by the public are the mainstay of university financing.

If they want to get their point of view across, let them take some trouble and not do it the easy way with demos and general disturbance. Let them get articles into the newspapers and magazines; let them use the university magazines and see that these get into the hands of the opinion formers and those who make the decisions. Let them not play to the least informed and unthinking section of the public and merely encourage their prejudices.

To end this chapter, I'd like to quote a "Parkinson's Law" that has a timeless application to university attitudes and activities. The redoubtable (and quirky) Professor C North-cote Parkinson very kindly fitted me into his very busy schedule and on his way from his home in Guernsey to India (this was in 1970); he spared me a few minutes at the West London Air Terminal and recorded this comment off the cuff:

To the university students of the world, my advice is: do not demonstrate. Whatever else you do, never demonstrate. This is a thing no university member, whether senior or junior, should ever do, because a demonstration in which students take part is a simple denial of everything for which the university stands. And I think it is briefly put in these words: that a slogan which is chanted a thousand times each by ten thousand people is, by university standards, no more likely to be right than the opposite opinion expressed, in a whisper, once – by one.

SOUTH AFRICA – THE WAY AHEAD

If you're not confused, you're not well informed

There is an ancient Spanish parable that goes something like this: "When God created Spain, He allowed the Spaniards three wishes. They chose to have the most varied climate in the world; the most beautiful women; and the most delicious foods and fruit and wine; and God agreed. But after a bit, they came back with a fourth wish – to have a good government. And God said "That is too much to ask."

I sense something of a parallel with our South African situation! The interesting speculation is "what might another government have done, given the complicated historical, ethnic and cultural mix in South Africa?" The question, of course, is unanswerable because there are far too many "permutations and complications" to be taken into account. Almost certainly there would still have been apartheid of a kind, but of an economic kind, between the "haves" and the "have nots", such as exists in other countries. There would still be those who had, as it were, bought their apartheid in advance and could remain economically and socially insulated from the effects of integration. These have always been among the sternest critics of the National Party government.

Inevitably, there has been talk – loosely bandied around by the armchair pundits both here and abroad – of "the coming revolution in South Africa". It is perhaps significant here to remember the famous words of the 19th century writer on political history, Alexis de Tocqueville, who commented on the French Revolution: "Patiently endured as long as it seemed beyond redress, a grievance comes to appear intolerable once the possibility of removing it crosses men's minds."

Meanwhile, State President P W Botha, amid all the shouting and the tumult and the clamour of nations telling South Africa what is good for it, has been trying to get on with the job of sorting out out a uniquely complex situation in an endeavour to achieve a modus vivendi for all South Africans, irrespective of colour. It might be suggested that, in an evolutionary manner, his track record is verging on the *re*volutionary. For one thing, he had done the unthinkable and split his National Party so that the die-hard conservative apartheidists tend to regard him as a left-wing subversive. He has also demonstrated a very important fact, that Afrikanerdom is not the monolithic stumbling block to "progress" as the world interprets the word. In the ranks of Afrikanerdom there has been a significant hiving away from the party line on the part of some politicians, academics and editors, among others.

In calling a general election (for White voters) in May 1987, the government was obviously seeking not only a renewed mandate for its reform policies, but also to test the strength of the right-wing opposition. The Conservative Party increased its support at the polls and has become the official opposition in Parliament, replacing the Progressive Federal Party, which lost heavily. The conservative opposition is a new factor and it remains to be seen what effect it will have on the reform processes.

Nevertheless, the increased number of Parliamentary seats now held by the National Party is a clear mandate for the government to press ahead with its policies. Still to be assessed as a factor is the increased support that it has received from the English-speaking section. Also, there is evidence pointing to increasing support from within the non-White communities in South Africa, though this is very difficult to gauge. The State President has laid stress on constitutionalism and gradualism, and also on the security of the state.

Although there was an apparent slowing down in the reform processes prior to the general election, much more had been achieved than the world gave credit for, and the changes have certainly not been only cosmetic. Now the time is ripe to accelerate the processes. One need that looms large is the further development of political structures that will give the Black population a meaningful say in affairs. (The Coloured and Indian communities already have their parliamentary representation in separate chambers).

Nevertheless, one has to view the current positive developments – the dismantling of apartheid and the winding down of restrictive legislation – against those very negative years when regulations that were nothing short of draconian pressed heavily on the non-White population. This is where the Afrikaner's strong sense of conformity and his rather unquestioning regard for authority (admirable up to a point) played him false and led to his being branded as insensitive and arrogant. There has been an aggravating factor in the existence within the public service of conservative elements who would not see any amelioration of or softening in the application of harsh laws as anything to do with them. One can unfortunately take this a step further with the suspicion that these same conservative elements (even at senior level) have not been unhappy to slow up the process of reform – a virtual sabotaging of government intentions.

There have been some very honourable exceptions in the case of those Afrikaners who were prepared to "break ranks" and express their honest objections to the system – and be ostracised for their pains. But, as I have tried to explain, history made the Afrikaner a very tribal person, and much as one might deplore the long silence for the most part of the Afrikaans churches to some of the injustices of the system, a knowledge of history will reveal the very distinctive and supportive rôle they were called upon to play in the Afrikaner's development.

In South Africa's political evolution, the English-speaking section of the population has tended to play an equivocal rôle. It is the interaction between the two major White groups that offers a key to some understanding of the South African situation as it is today. (The historical aspects of

this relationship was dealt with in the chapter *Boer and Brit*).
I think it is unfortunate that my section, the English-speakers, has embraced rather many what I call part-time liberals,
those who have enjoyed the comforts and conveniences of
apartheid but have not gone out of their way to improve
conditions and yet have been quick to damn the government. This led best-seller Afrikaans novelist and critic
André Brink (some of his books are available in English
translation) to comment on the rôle of the English-speaking
South African. Let me say that Brink is not a member of the
Afrikaans "establishment"; in fact, he tends to be frowned
upon in those circles because of his free and "liberal" thinking and writing. Some years ago, he referred to " ... those
English-speaking South Africans who have hypocritically
chosen to 'dissociate' themselves and to be patronising
about 'the corruption of power' and the political naïveté of
backvelders (a reference to the rural background of many
Afrikaners). Without the possibility of offering an alternative government, they found it easy to be 'liberal'. Safely
entrenched behind their swimming pools and lawns and
their host of underpaid and immaculately liveried servants,
they have become the true colonial Tories. How could they
understand the process of Afrikaans thinking?"

Strong stuff, and certainly not applicable in all instances
and, these days, to a large extent outdated. But it is difficult
to repress the feeling that my section of White South Africa
has confounded the political situation; it has even been said
that we couldn't have done better had we had a master plan
to work ourselves out of power.

This is easy to say in retrospect, being wise after the
event. The alternatives were not so apparent and, among
other factors, electoral constituencies were "loaded" in
favour of the rural voter (where the strength of Afrikanerdom lay). The English section was active and successful in
industry and commerce, while the other section beavered
their way into the civil service and other positions of influence. The civil service became very largely Afrikanerised,
with potential recruits from the other section saying that
they saw no future for an English-speaker. This was really

not so, although it must be admitted that in the earlier days of National Party government (after 1948), there were instances of gross discrimination. The situation, however, improved progressively.

The English-language press has played a big part in conditioning the English-speaker. It fulminated against the government, it gave very little credit when credit was due; such ameliorations of policy as did happen were often criticised as "the Nats going back on their policy". The end result was that, as long as you were anti-Nat, your conscience was clear. It has been a saying in South Africa about supporters of the erstwhile opposition in Parliament: "They vote Prog (the Progressive Federal Party) but they thank God for the Nats".

It could seem that I am "piling it on a bit" against the English-speaking South African. This is not my intention; after all, I am one of them. And there are many, many exceptions to whatever strictures might be levelled. But, as I have already implied, my section has tended – albeit unwittingly perhaps – to allow the Afrikaner to "carry the can back", that is to say we have happily cast on his shoulders responsibility for all the sins of omission and commission in a dauntingly complex situation. To me, this is unfair, and furthermore it provided false perceptions of South Africa to the outside world. No society, or group within that society, is without its hypocrisies, but even at the risk of generalising, it seems to me that our group could have been doing more in individual and corporate ways to ease the social burden of non-Whites without it always being implied as a criticism of the Nats. After all, whatever the government in power, the exploding Black population had to be educated, trained for jobs, housed, employed, cared for medically and provided with other social services. Admittedly there was a lot of unpublished good done by individuals and organisations over the years, but even in those instances in which private initiative could have found solutions or just "got on with the job", there was a pervading attitude "why doesn't the government do something about it?" Certainly there were things that only the government could do, but, as in now evident, the private sector can be a very good motivator – and often a more efficient one. One could say that there has been a tendency to be more preoccupied with the politics of the problem than the problem itself.

One noteworthy exception has been the Urban Foundation which came into being in 1977 and is still guided by its founding fathers – Harry Oppenheimer, then chairman of the giant Anglo-American Corporation; Dr Anton Rupert, chairman of the Rembrandt industrial empire, and executive director Jan Steyn, former Supreme Court judge. It has concerned itself with improving conditions for urban Black communities in the way of housing, education, health and community facilities. Its achievements up to now have been praiseworthy, although, odd as it may seem, its efforts have not met with unanimous favour within the Black communities where a feeling persists that unless an organisation makes a political stand, it is ineffective. Political involvement, as far as the Foundation is concerned is just not on. In fact, at the meeting convened to establish the Foundation, Mr Oppenheimer stressed that a distinction had to be made between political problems and those that fell within the ambit of the private sector.

Mining groups have now also been moved to do something about the disputed migrant labour system by embarking on massive housing schemes for black mineworkers so that they can have their families with them. An organisation like Anglo-American is talking in terms of 24 000 low-cost houses to be built on mine properties and adjacent land bought for the purpose.

Looking back, it is interesting to reflect just how well or badly South Africa has been served by traditional parliamentary methods. You will have read Salvador de Madariaga's comments in the chapter headed *One Man One Vote* and there have been many voices expressing doubt about the efficacy of the Westminster system in environments other than the one in which it was born. It has had very doubtful success in other parts of Africa, so why should it necessarily be considered the answer in South Africa? It may be an heretical thought, but can a country which is both First-world and Third-world (with the latter predominating) afford the luxury of this inherited system? In a country which has such enormous problems of development and inter-group adjustments – socially, economically and politically, as well as establishing its rôle in Southern Africa – a traditional form of opposition that lays stress more on matters that are divisive and cause conflict rather than common matters and consensus opportunities might rightfully be regarded with suspicion. Here again the media play an important part, not to withhold information but to point to the potential for consensus and cooperation.

The former parliamentary opposition played its orthodox part, but over its many years in the parliamentary wilderness, with no real prospect of taking over the reins of government, it became rather like the man who cried "wolf" too often. One wonders whether, without the sniping and the point-scoring, South Africa by now might have been further on the road to genuine reform. One result on the overemphasis on divisiveness by elements of the press has been to breed suspicion on the part of those very people which the reform processes aim to help. Historian Daniel Boorstin made the point:

Disagreement is the life blood of democracy, dissension its cancer. Disagreers seek solutions to common problems, dissenters seek power for themselves.

Meanwhile, South Africa's judiciary, although it has no option but to work within the statutes (sometimes challenging them effectively) has played a very honourable rôle in upholding civil liberties.

Now, in 1987, quo vadis? As in making love and making war, and in the practice of politics, timing is of the essence. South Africa has tended to indulge in what might be termed "reactive politics", that is to say reacting to events rather than anticipating them. Henry Kissinger once observed that history is kind to political leaders who use a margin of choice while it is still available and that those who wait on events are usually overwhelmed by them. When it comes to the international arena, there is no option but to keep up with the inescapable realities of the world at large, one of which is a universal abhorrence of institutionalised racial politics as seen to be practised in South Africa, irrespective of any positive aspects that may have been implicit in them. It remains ironic that nominal possession of so-called "political rights" has meant so little to so many millions of the world's population in their material welfare and happiness. Political self-determination without economic independence means very little.

In my view, South Africa has "got the message", albeit tardily. It has recognised that bending economics to the total philosophy of separate development has put us into unnecessarily heavy debt and brought about a monstrously top-heavy and expensive public service with a multiplicity of controls that overrode market considerations. The private sector which has tended to wait on government action has been stimulated to get on with whatever it can do to improve social conditions and introduce non-Whites into the free enterprise system, as well as to set productivity goals to match rapidly rising non-White wages and salaries. I visited a gold mine in the Transvaal recently and was very struck with the wages for Black mineworkers that were quoted to me; they would be an eye-opener for those critics abroad who believe that the South African economy is supported on the backs of slave labour. Furthermore, legislation is being put through Parliament to open job categories in the mining industry to all race groups, many of them having hitherto been reserved for Whites. Yet another nail in the apartheid coffin.

In recent years, there has been a rapid spread of trade unionism, officially recognised, among South Africa's Black workers. This is a problem area because the reciprocities involved in trade unionism (that is, the proper relationship between employer and employee) and the inescapable economic parameters within which commerce and industry operate are not fully recognised on the workers' side. This is understandable because, like the Westminster system of democracy, the concept is entirely foreign to Black tradition and thereby lends itself to abuse. To be fair, the example offered by some White unions abroad has not been laudable.

What has happened is that Black unions have become politicised, which of course is nothing new, but in the South African context it is prejudicial to those very people whom it is intended to benefit. Black trade unionism is being drawn into the "liberation struggle", and what should be the immediate concern of Black trade unionists, to wit wages and working conditions, is being subverted by radicals into militant action in the form of strikes and intimidation which, even in the short term, can only penalise the workers. The radicals will still have their assured sources of income, but thousands of Black families will be suffering. I doubt whether the situation is comprehended abroad because of the unthinking tendency to regard all countries as similar and all peoples as having the same motivation. Some of the Black strikers even expect to be paid by the employer while on strike. Certainly, at this present stage, ill-considered industrial action by trade union leaders could lead to the introduction of increased mechanisation by employers with a consequent loss of jobs – a further penalising of workers' interests.

However, the fact that the miners' strike in the second half of 1987 (which involved several hundred thousand Blacks) was settled by negotiation in a matter of weeks is a significant pointer to a more reasonable and understanding approach to industrial affairs and augurs well for the future of negotiation in other spheres.

A new element has now entered the employment picture – what might be termed "participatory capitalism". An increasing number of companies (including some of the "giants") are in process of offering their Black employees shares in the respective companies. Elsewhere in the world, this giving workers a stake in the progress of the company has already proved a powerful stimulus, and, as a local newspaper put it, "a forceful challenge to ideologies which are too inflexible to meet changing circumstances".

But, with all these positive advances, the final political alignment has still to be determined. The world wants a quick "fix" ... get the African National Congress to the negotiation table and all will fall into place ... release Nelson Mandela and all will be well. As the world should know, Mandela has been offered his release on humanitarian grounds on condition that he renounces violence. But how many people have considered whether it perhaps suits his and the ANC book for him to remain in gaol as "a martyr to the cause"? And perhaps he feels safer where he is for the time being, considering the turbulence and violence of Black politics. Certainly he is well accommodated and under no physical duress as his visitors, both local and from abroad, can testify.

It is significant that an article in *Le Figaro* commented on the naïveté of certain Western leaders who will not believe that the ANC (however innocent its beginnings) is now controlled by Communists. In South Africa, there are members of the Black community who have to rid themselves of the belief that the attainment of political power will bring about their economic millennium; they only have to look north to independent Africa to realise that this is a non-starter. The great mass of the population will not be living in the posh suburbs and driving expensive cars.

One hears a lot about "liberation movements", but the question needs to be asked whether the masses have been liberated or whether power has merely moved into less efficient and more corrupt hands. Like democracy, liberation has become a corrupted word. It would be helpful all round if the world were to show more regard for semantics and not go along with what has become known as Afro-jargon.

Here are some examples:

aggressors   racists, imperialists, colonialists, former colonialists, neo-colonialists etc. but excluding communists.

democracy	rule by Blacks
freedom fighter	terrorist
guerilla	freedom fighter, but if he has any Western connections, then defined as a brutal murderer.
reform	handing over power lock stock and barrel to Blacks.
genuine South African reform	final transfer of power to the South African Communist Party or a radical left power clique.
racist	someone who is not on the left/liberal/Marxist side
sanctions	punishment for racists. This does not prevent those advocating sanctions from trading under the counter with these same "racists".

There has been a sort of hijacking of vocabulary by the liberal-left (and not least the Marxists) that found reflection in the comments of an observer at the Trades Union Congress in Brighton in September 1984: "I received the impression that in the semi-literate vocabulary of the New Labour Movement, 'violence' has come to mean any action by employers or government of which it disapproves – from shortening a tea break to closing a factory, from wondering about the need for universal family benefits to membership of NATO."

Another word that has been hijacked, in a manner of speaking, is democracy. Modern usage has given it the restricted meaning of one-man-one-vote in a unitary state, but this is not its basic meaning which is, in simple terms, government by the people. What is important to acknowledge is that the form that this government should take is not prescribed, and this has been implicit in earlier chapters of this book, including the views of Salvador de Madariaga quoted in the second chapter.

The world would be doing Africa a great service if it were to inject into its attitudes to, and its relationship with, this continent a healthy dose of realism. But again, in the received wisdom of the left, the realist is regarded as something of a screaming right-winger, a reactionary, even a fascist. The world should be much readier to use a good old-fashioned expletive that has eight letters beginning with "b" and ending with "t". (It is often condensed to the first four letters, beginning with "b" and ending with a double "l").

The West should realise that it is indulging – quite unconsciously perhaps – in a form of what I might term "reverse racism". It has long regarded in an indulgent light the foibles (to put it kindly) that have been a feature of African affairs for so many years. Is this not tacitly saying "Well, what else can you expect of them?" This, I would maintain, is racism in a pernicious form because it distorts value judgments and prejudices rational thinking – and also preserves the climate for continuing moral blackmail. The West could do with a great deal less of the mealy-mouthed talk that it has cultivated over the years for fear of appearing "racist". Being sympathetic does not have to involve throwing commonsense overboard.

There is much talk of a new constitution for South Africa, but it is interesting to note what a former Professor of Public Law at the University of Cape Town wrote some time back:

There is a tendency in South Africa to regard constitutional dispensations as "solutions" rather than as devices which both reflect and influence continuing political processes. The fact that there is no "quick fix solution" to the South African dilemma then inevitably leads to the rejection of constitutional government as unrealistic, a conclusion backed up by reference to the history of post-independent Anglophonic Africa.

The truth of the matter is that constitutions do not solve political problems. They can, however, be a part, and an important part, of a political process by which such problems may be resolved. Their rôle need not be purely passive. They can provide the mechanisms and values which constitute the context for political change and thus influence its direction.

114

So, there is reason for South Africa moving slowly, despite the logjam having largely been broken. A factor that has to be taken into account is the decision-making arising from the existence of a number of consultative bodies – and this is inevitably time-consuming. In the meantime, slogans will continue to masquerade as political thought both here and abroad, but armchair critics will have to accept that politics is the art of the possible. Also, they will have to accept that there will be no comprehensive reform without stability.

Pope John XXIII, in his encyclical *Pacem in Terris*, proclaimed these thoughts:

It must be borne in mind that to proceed gradually is the law of life in all its expressions.

Therefore, in human institutions, too, it is not possible to renovate for the better except by working from within them, gradually ... Violence has always achieved only destruction, not construction, the kindling of passions, not their pacification, the accumulation of hate and ruin and not the reconciliation of the contending parties. And it has reduced men and parties to the difficult task of rebuilding, after sad experience, on the ruins of discord.

We in South Africa need to get our point of view across to the world better than we have up to now. One important aspect is that we are in a state of transition that can go on for years. People abroad should forget about this "quick fix" nostrum and realise that their attitudes can play a part in the creation of the proper climate for a post-apartheid South African society. They might start by demanding from South Africa's adversaries the same pure democratic values that they now expect from Pretoria.

Taking into account the influence of the media, and perhaps at the risk of seeming facetious, I have had in mind for years what could be a very interesting experiment, to wit the introduction of something that, for want of a better term, I will call a "media moratorium" ... close it all down for an experimental month and let the world simmer down to a less frenetic and emotional state! Absurdly impractical,

115

of course, but perhaps you sense the gist of the thought behind it. I can only say again that we all need to understand better how the media work, that every branch of the media is to all intents and purposes selling a product, and it behoves us to recognise a shoddy product when we come upon one. Elements of the media are adept at playing on concealed aggressions and prejudices, but apart from this, the news selected for presentation is seldom the rounded picture. It was put rather well by a young British writer, Matthew Heald Cooper, in his most recent novel *Dog Eats Dog* (Victor Gollancz, London 1986) which opens with these words:

For journalists, that second Saturday in December was a quiet day. They found no spectacular news on the international scene, and had to be content with a terrorist attack in the Lebanon, seventeen killed, continuing protests in Poland over price rises, and yet another guerilla offensive in El Salvador. In Africa, a riot had left 400 dead in the streets, but it was the wrong part of the continent – in a country ruled by blacks not whites, and with no photo-opportunities – so it hardly merited a column; a famine elsewhere killing a thousand a day had been going on too long for notice. In all, the sum of human suffering seemed set to remain unaltered for the next twenty-four hours, so that the men on the news desks put their feet up disgruntledly, and only the death of an alcoholic film-star saved their lives from utter tedium ...

Inevitably, for some time to come, South Africa will remain a useful target for people of all persuasions to focus their latent aggressions on, their holier-than-thou attitudes, their cynicisms and sophistries, their selective indignation.

Well-known Soviet dissident Anatoly Shcharansky, in an address given in the United States in the early part of 1987, said "The West praises the Soviet Union when it makes progress as far as human rights are concerned, but when South Africa does something similar it is unacceptable and it is threatened with sanctions." One might imagine that Mr Shcharansky's "liberal" credentials are good enough for weight to be given to his views. But moral standpoints remain one of the casualties of the international scene. We need many more people abroad with the courage of their convictions to accept that there are many more regimes more repressive than South Africa's. And we're doing something about it!

Looking to the future, South Africans are independent people who don't take kindly to being pushed around, even verbally, particularly by those whom we suspect of having an axe to grind. A well-publicised anti-apartheid stance can be used not only for political ends but as a market strategy to penetrate and capture new markets.

We in South Africa were not exactly taken in by the sanctions recommendations that came from the so-called Eminent Persons Group appointed by a Commonwealth Conference in the Bahamas to visit South Africa and to report; two at least of its members who spoke in favour of sanctions were from countries nicely positioned to take over some of South Africa's long-established markets – and to hell with the fact that tens of thousands of South African Blacks would lose their jobs.

It was a further irony, after the high moral aura surrounding the EPG and its investigations into the iniquities of the South African system, that it most highly-profiled member, former Australian Prime Minister Malcolm Fraser, should have been "caught with his pants down". According to reports from Memphis, Tennessee, he was found in the early hours of the morning in a hotel lobby minus his trousers. The explanation proffered from Australia was that Mr Fraser's drinks were "spiked" by a South African secret agent. This strikes one as more Hollywood than Memphis!

We in South Africa would like fewer lectures from abroad and more conversations.

We don't trust those who prescribe solutions that bear little relation to the situation as it really is, nor are we keen to be "sold down the river" as has happened before in Africa. We don't like the goal posts to be shifted at the world's whim.

117

We are aware of these maxims attributed to Abraham Lincoln:

You cannot strengthen the weak by weakening the strong.

You cannot help small men by tearing down big men.

You cannot help the poor by destroying the rich.

You cannot help the wage earner by pulling down the wage payer.

You cannot further the brotherhood of man by inciting class hatred.

You cannot build character and courage by taking away a man's initiative and independence.

You cannot help men permanently by doing for them what they could and should do for themselves.

Accepting these dicta, South Africans and others need to be careful about overdrawing their emotional bank accounts. However admirable their intentions may be, the "bleeding hearts brigade" have no place in the complexities of our society. I am referring to those who are always wringing their hands over the inequalities that exist in society ... and in this way South Africa is far from being unique. I admit that we do offer some grave instances but not all of these are due to heartlessness. If, say, an unskilled labourer (of any colour skin) elects to have a dozen children and as a result of his low earnings these children are ill-clad and sometimes hungry, is "society" to blame? The question needs to be asked and answered. By all means try to do something to ameliorate the hardship, but to wallow in self-criticism is self-defeating.

Fortunately, we do not have too many cases such as that of Mr Msisinyani Sam Magomani who died in Gazankulu in the early part of 1987 at the age of 84, leaving 19 wives and 50 children!

With the substantial pool of goodwill still existing between the various population groups in our country, I see South Africa coming through this period of adjustment greatly strengthened. Most of us can already discern a much greater degree of awareness of what our country really needs, of the hopes and desires of all population groups, and a growing ambition to see these realised, even at some sacrifice. Because of the colossal disinformation campaign to which we are subjected, overseas people don't realise how comparatively fast the process is moving. At home we tend to complain about the slowness of the reform processes, but in doing so we forget that the State President cannot move too far ahead of public opinion when there are ultra-conservative rightists waiting on every opportunity to gather more support. This is something that even President Botha's critics, let alone the party in power, would not wish to see happen. Much as many of us feel that the time has come for bold action, the words of President Wilson are still timely. He once wrote:

> The ear of the leader must ring with the voices of the people. He cannot be of the school of the prophets; he must be of the number of those who serve the slow-paced daily need.

There is much more inter-group consultation these days in every sphere of life. We are becoming more aware of what the other man thinks. Critics should not shut their eyes to the probability that the constitutional probings that are going on could lead to the implementation of a system under which South Africans of colour would achieve a much more meaningful say in their affairs. As indicated earlier in this chapter, the process has already started with the Coloured and Indian communities which have their own chambers in Parliament with ministerial representation in the previously all-White Cabinet.

Another recent development is the institution of Regional Services Councils which are joint multi-racial local authorities, one of whose priorities is to see that underdeveloped areas within their jurisdiction get their fair share of the development "cake".

The promulgation of a National Council is a further step towards achieving multi-racial representation at high level. It has been described by the Minister of Constitutional Development and Planning as "one of the most fundamental reform steps that this government, or any other government, has yet taken in the history of our country". However,

it has to be realised that these are constitutional probes conducted in a very sensitive society and political climate and that there are those who will set out to wreck them. Anyone who has the interests of all South Africans at heart would be well advised to look into the motivations and credentials of these potential wreckers. To quote Daniel Boorstin again:
... Disagreers seek solutions to common problems, dissenters seek power for themselves.

One possible constitutional solution that has cropped up in discussion from time to time has been crystallised by the recent publication of a book *South Africa: the Solution* by a husband-and-wife team Leon Louw and Frances Kendall (Amagi Publications, Bisho, Ciskei). It has become a best-seller in the short time since it was published. The book cites a Swiss-style confederation with a central government of limited powers and a variety of local authorities that would enable South Africans of all colours to choose the economic and social system under which they would prefer to live. There is much more to it, of course, and the book certainly adds constructively to the mix of argument and discussion taking place.

On this score, one could recall the situation in the United States during the civil rights agitation. George F Kennan, a former United States ambassador to the Soviet Union and university professor and considered at the time to be one of America's foremost thinkers, said that he was aware of Black leaders who were themselves advocating local political communities where their people could express themselves collectively and gain both authority and responsibility.

This found an echo in Arthur M Schlesinger Jr's book *The Crisis of Confidence* (from which I quoted earlier in this book) which dealt with the civil rights campaign in the United States in the 1960's. Schlesinger wrote:
Most promising of all, from the viewpoint of direct participation, is the Robert Kennedy model which involves not a resort to the state and municipal political units that had so long toadied to the local moguls but the creation

120

of 'new community institutions that local residents control and through which they can express their wishes'. Such new institutions, Kennedy hoped, could build 'self-sufficiency and self-determination within the communities of poverty', help the poor shape their own destiny and bring 'not just individual residents but the entire community into the mainstream of American life'...

Schlesinger goes on to say:

Decentralisation can easily become, as with the New Right and the New Left, a demagogic crusade against the national government. But the New Politics, I take it, would join decentralisation with a wise use of the national authority. This could well lead to a burst of administrative and institutional invention that could do much to combat the conviction of powerlessness in the high-technology society and to bring all our citizens into vital relation with the national community. And, if we deny all legitimate demand for reasonable participation, we are going to force the passion for participation into illegitimate and destructive outlets.

"Administrative and institutional invention" I see as a highly significant phrase, and it could be applied to the deliberations of the KwaZulu-Natal Indaba that met to thresh out a more meaningful community existence for the people of Natal Province and the self-governing territory of KwaZulu which originally formed part of the Province. (Indaba is a Zulu word signifying a getting together for the discussion of important matters). Its proposals could be described as inventive, imaginative – and practical, but initial reaction from the government was cautious, although it has admitted that the Indaba "is on the right track". However, the subsequent proclamation of the Joint Executive Authority for Natal and KwaZulu has been described by the Administrator of Natal as "the dawn of a new and interesting period" in cooperation.

About the Indaba, the distinguished South African Alan Paton wrote in the Anglo-American/de Beers prestige monthly journal *Optima*:

A total or near total rejection of the Indaba proposals by the ruling party would be a calamity. The total or near acceptance would give hope to many who despair of the future. If a new province of Natal should become … an example of a successful non-racial government, it might inspire the people of South Africa to set up Indabas of their own, and so open the way to the creation of a federal Republic of South Africa, which many believe to be not only the sensible constitutional solution of our most complex problems, but an alternative to the unitary state that they so fear.

In this context, it might be noted that the idea of federation in South Africa is not new. It goes back into the last century, and on the eve of Union in 1910, the celebrated South African writer Olive Schreiner wrote several lengthy letters to the newspaper *The Transvaal Leader* advocating a federation of the Cape Colony, Natal, the Transvaal and the Orange Free State instead of union.

On the subject of the unitary state ("one man one vote, and winner takes all") a letter to the editor of the Cape Town *Argus* newspaper makes an intriguing point. It suggests that the current desire to bring South Africa to its knees before "liberation" is inspired by the fear that if South Africa were economically and in other ways too strong when "liberation" came, South African Blacks would pose a threat to their (Black) neighbours! We have our Gilbert and Sullivan situations here, too.

It is an exciting time for us, with tremendous developments on the horizon. Unrest has declined substantially, and there are great opportunities for all South Africans to seize, not least the non-White who, in large numbers, is moving steadily into a middle-class stratum and taking a much greater share of the economic cake. In fact, it has been said by an overseas observer that there are more Black-owned vehicles in South Africa than there are private motor cars in the whole of Soviet Russia.

All remaining disparities in pay and service conditions

between population groups in the public service are being eliminated.

Blacks are steadily moving into managerial positions, even over Whites, and there is already a proliferation of Black-owned businesses trading freely, and the small-business idea ("every man his own boss") is rapidly on the rise. There will be a vast expansion in service industries to help absorb the pool of labour available.

A question to be asked is whether those from abroad who pay lightning official "fact finding" visits to Africa and then prescribe what is good for South Africa know anything about the real Africa, not the propaganda Africa. One has a suspicion that they are very often misled by the camouflage of the Mercedes-Benz cavalcade at the airport and other elaborate trappings (both possibly paid for by foreign aid). I am not sure that I wouldn't personally side with the reply of Sir Roy Welensky (Prime Minister of the wrecked Federation of Rhodesia and Nyasaland) when asked by a supercilious television interviewer whether he claimed to know the African mind: "Considering that when I was a lad I swam bare-arsed in the Makabusi with the piccanins, I think I can say that I know something about Africans."

Visitors who come to see the South Africa situation for themselves should avoid getting locked in with self-serving politicians and try to see South African in the round. A walk through the streets among the ordinary people and time spent in a supermarket to see what people are buying are revealing activities. The contents of supermarket trolleys pushed by members of our non-White communities could be very illuminating and positive proof of the extent to which income levels have risen among these communites. I hope it is not too cynical-seeming – on the score of this greater affluence – to choose this point to note the warning that has come from the Medical Research Council of South Africa that the country should gear itself for a heart disease epidemic in the Black population similar to that among the Whites.

As I implied earlier, we South Africans are a little tired of the "observers" from abroad who come to our country and have meetings with a limited number of carefully pre-selected contacts, clearly signalling "My mind is made up, don't confuse me with facts". The focus of these visitors is most often largely set on politics, but politics is not an out-right priority for the ordinary people in a society. Many other considerations apply in assessing the true nature of a country. Political activists tend to rock the boat for those who are not really basically interested, and, what is more, they risk alienating the sympathy and patience and toler-ance of otherwise well-intentioned people.

There are, of course, many agreeable "exceptions to the rule" among the "observers" who come to this country. I remember a senior woman from the BBC who came out to see for herself what South Africa was all about. I showed her some hospitality, and she asked me to recommend any people who, in my opinion, would give her an accurate pic-ture. One of those I suggested was the editor of the Cape Town Afrikaans daily *Die Burger,* and I rang him up as an old contact and asked whether he could see her. She sub-sequently told me that, of all her contacts in South Africa, this Afrikaans editor had given her a far truer picture, in her assessment, than any other, including (and she named them) certain prominent "liberals" in Johannesburg.

One thorny aspect that still has to be resolved is the appli-cation of the Group Areas Act – the separation of residential areas, schools etc. on a racial basis. This has been a key-stone of the policy of separate development (remember – that was what apartheid was all about) and with statements from the government side that apartheid is being disman-tled, the future of the Act is being more and more called into question. True, there have been relaxations already, but this is another instance where minority rights are a factor that cannot lightly be swept away. Those cases in which overseas companies doing business in South Africa and who appoint Blacks in senior positions with accommodation pro-vided in designated "White" areas make interesting test cases.

124

There is an infinite number of examples of non-discrimination that the world knows nothing about because that is not "the popular line" as far as the overseas media are concerned.

To take other examples that touch me as an individual, I have recently come back from a documentary film shoot on which we had a young Black camera assistant. There was no discrimination between us; we all stayed in the same hotels and ate together in the same restaurants – there was no differentiation.

I am an asthma sufferer and attend the respiratory clinic at the famous Groote Schuur hospital where I have access to the most sophisticated medical equipment to be found anywhere. The great majority of outpatients who share these facilities with me are non-White.

I remember some years ago doing a radio feature on the Red Cross War Memorial Children's Hospital which is not very far away from Groote Schuur where the world's first human heart transplant was performed. The Red Cross hospital also has a high reputation for heart surgery, and I well remember visiting the open-heart surgery ward and seeing six beds each with a small figure surrounded by masses of equipment. These were six children who had undergone surgery that morning and only one of them was White. The youngest patient was the child of a Coloured shepherd in the Beaufort West district of the Cape. Based on the father's low earnings, the fees that would be charged to him for this most sophisticated operation on his child would be precisely nil.

Much the same thing will apply to the Black Siamese twins in Johannesburg. The operation to separate them will be most complicated because they are joined at the head, and a team of no fewer than 40 medical personnel will be involved. Provided there are no complications, the procedures will take from six weeks to two months to complete. And the fee to be levied? It has already been assessed. From time of admission to time of discharge the fee will be R10 – the equivalent of US $5. We do well by our sick people in this country, irrespective of colour.

Just in passing, one of the most highly rated shows on television among all South Africans is "The Cosby Show" featuring Black American comedian Bill Cosby – despite the fact that he says he doesn't like apartheid! Which makes nonsense of the claim by a Black actor in Britain, in supporting Equity's ban on the sale to South Africa of radio and television programmes, that British television companies would conspire not to use Black artistes to make sure their programmes would be saleable in the (lucrative) South African market. The radical activists seldom do their homework, it seems, because a glance at South African television screens would reveal that Black actors and actresses abound in American shows, including all-Black casts like "The Cosby Show".

Incidentally, I am given to believe (on what I take to be good authority) that the Afrikaans newspaper *Die Burger* mentioned earlier has more non-Whites on its editorial staff than *The New York Times* has Blacks.

Another pointer – our Human Sciences Research Council (government sponsored) has just come out with a report suggesting that African languages should be a compulsory examination subject in White primary schools.

These are significant shifts, one could almost call them dramatic, and they are steadily increasing. It augurs well for the future.

In government and parastatal organisations there is going to be a much greater concentration on what the real priorities of the country are. At the news conference after the business summit convened by the State President in November 1986, it was announced that the government's spending policy had shifted from large-scale infrastructure development to socio-economic development. This included such programmes as the accelerated building of schools as part of a seven-fold increase in spending on Black education, and a massive housing programme.

I look forward to the time (perhaps not so far away) when emotions have cooled; when the world has become less of a busybody; when the assorted shibboleths that have been assiduously spread by propagandists no longer hold with those who are concerned with the real world; when silliness no longer gains acceptance as moral concern as, for instance, in the row that broke out over the display in the American Museum of Natural History of fossils from South Africa, acknowledgedly one of the richest areas in the world; when pragmatism and rationality have once again come to the fore.

I see South Africa eventually restored to its rightful place in the community of nations as a natural leader in southern Africa, a member of the OAU (the Organisation of African Unity), and an example to the world of how a very mixed community at differing stages of development can live together in reasonable prosperity and amity. I see a big influx of immigrants, new South Africans wanting to share in the exciting things that are happening in this power house of the south, and wanting to enjoy some of the pleasures of living in this sunny land, with its mountains and its beaches, its vineyards and its orchards ... they will follow the thousands upon thousands of British, Dutch, German, Portuguese, Greek, Italian and people of other nations who already find South Africa a fine country in which to live and work.

Impossible dream? I don't think so.

I want to end this chapter with something that, in a light-hearted way, captures something of the essence of what South Africa means to us – when we are not being too serious. That stylish magazine titled, appropriately *Style*, published an amusing list headed "101 Reasons for Staying in South Africa" and followed it up a few months later with another list of 101 good reasons. Here are some examples:

America is full of people who say "Have a nice day" when they couldn't care less if you dropped dead.

The rest of the world doesn't deserve us.

There are 50 000 kinds of fly in Australia.

Who wants to be known as a South African boat person?

127

No one overseas recognises the worth of my John Meyer original

South Africa has the best-run game reserves in the world. We have to stay for the sake of the animals.

Biltong

Luke and Andrew are down for Michaelhouse and it's too late to try for Eton.

How on earth would one cope without the ritual white guilt complex?

Highveld storms and jacarandas.

Australia is full of Australians.

Australia is full of South Africans.

Churches whose leading figures are a constant source of entertainment.

Klein dorps with names like Pofadder and Putsonderwater.

Castle Lager

England is damp, crowded, expensive, highly competitive, and the Labour Party might take over.

All the Russian nuclear missiles are aimed at America or Europe.

South Africa has beaches and waves. Europe has pebbles and pools, all of which are crowded and polluted.

We would not be eligible for new driver's licences. (We'd never be able to unlearn all our bad driving habits)

We'd get corrupted reading all that pornography they have over there.

Gambling odds on Sun City slot machines are better than almost anywhere else in the world.

SAA is one of the safest airlines in the world.

The Drakensberg.

If we go, who's going to give the blacks jobs?

The BIG Turffontein jackpot.

Elephants

The only man in the world who understands your hair has his salon in Rosebank.

You get travelsick.

The smell of dust rising from dirt roads.

The Blue Train

Cape crayfish and perlemoen
Cape coloured humour.
What problem?
What would the rest of the world do without us to criticise and show what good liberals they are?
The Americans drive on the wrong side of the road.
Granny can't get her money out.
You can't get Granny out.
Queen and Elton John have promised never to play Sun City again.
By process of elimination, you stand a good chance of being chairman of Anglo-American within the next few years.
Kangaroos stink.
You're indispensable.
You're in detention.
Imagine missing the chance of finally getting to know black South Africans.
You're P W Botha.
You're Nelson Mandela.
South Africa's full of South Africans. They're not bad buggers after all, you know.

* * * * * *

"I sometimes think that God had something left over and emptied His pocket over the southern continent ... He scattered on South Africa not only gold and diamonds and other minerals but beauty and something to appeal to the human spirit."

... General Smuts.